Here I Am Again

(A Call to Persistent Praying)

Here I Am Again

A Call to Persistent Praying

Tofunmi Akinyemi

Jochebed Publishing House
Akure. Ondo State. Nigeria.

Presented to

____

By

____

On

____

"... men always ought to pray and not loose heart..." Luke 18:1.

"Pray without ceasing."
1 Thessalonians 5:17.

"Trust in Him at all times... pour out your heart to Him; God is a refuge for us."
Psalm 62:8.

Dedication

Thankfully dedicated **to the Almighty GOD.**

Table of Content

APPENDIX

Acknowledgement

My heartfelt praise is to the Almighty God for saving my soul, and for preserving me in the Christian race. I thank God for the gift of life, the treasured privilege to be His child; to be usable of Him, and for helping me to write this book.

Immense gratitude to the Awesome God for His amazing love for me; for His faithfulness, goodness, kindness, and mercy. Thank You Lord God Almighty for Your Victory and Glory; thank You for everything. Indeed, in the words of Chris Tomlin, "You are a Good, Good, Father"! I am eternally grateful.

I appreciate my husband, Kola, and all our children; for their unflinching support over the years. Surely, our reward shall be sweet at the coming of our Lord and Saviour Jesus Christ.

A big thanks to Tomiwo Akinyemi for proof-reading this work; and for his constructive criticisms. I thank the Ministry's Staff, and all who have supported the Ministry over the years; for their contributions to the fulfilment of God's purpose for my life. God bless us all in Jesus Christ's Name, Amen.

I am grateful to Tosin Akinyemi (Esq.) for his useful suggestions in the course of writing this Book; also, Heart of Words, U.K. for the cover design; and Esthom Graphic Prints, Ibadan, for the printing work. Best wishes of God's blessings to you and yours in Jesus Name, Amen.

"Now unto the King eternal, immortal, invisible, the only wise God, be honour and glory forever and ever." 1 Timothy 1:17.

Tofunmi Akinyemi
(Mama Jochebed).

Preamble

The Genesis of this Book

The title and inspiration for this Book (Here I am again) came from a discussion I had with a young man whom I choose to refer to as "Christian".

Christian shared with me (among other things) the testimony of how God answered his prayers concerning a dire need in his life. During the waiting period, he regularly went to the Almighty God in prayers saying:

"Baba, mo tun de o, oro mi yi naa ni o ….". (Yoruba; an indigenous language of the South West, Nigeria).

That is, Father, here I am again, it is all about this my issue …."

Christian made supplications to God in the Name of Jesus Christ. He trusted God to arise for his help, and was expectant! God did show up for Christian, and made it happen for him in the very nick of time.

The Almighty God did for Christian what He alone could do. Christian's testimony is sealed with the precious Blood of Jesus Christ, Amen.

Another source of inspiration for this book came from a playlet written by the above-mentioned "Christian". It centred on who the Christian is in Christ; and the exceedingly great provisions made available to Christians through Jesus Christ!

It challenges Christians to disallow satan from "robbing" us of our privileges in Christ. Also, that we should regularly appropriate the victory of the Cross as the need arises on life's path.

This Book

The Book "Here I am Again" is about persistent praying, and the power in the Name of Jesus Christ. Also about having a stubborn faith in God in the face of seemingly impossible situations; totally depending on Him, and trusting Him in all His dealings with us; even when we sometimes don't understand.

It talks about the weapons of our warfare, and remaining steadfast in our Christian walk. It is about being at peace during life's storms, and seeing the reality of God's "Victory and Glory"; even in the waiting period before the miracle!

The truth of God's Word in this Book will quicken your spirit, and awaken the warrior in you. It will fire you up to pray continually, and thereby regularly take possession of all that God has for you and your generation.

Each Chapter of this Book represents an essential ingredient for effective praying; except Chapters Twenty-six and Twenty-seven which are messages of assurance and salvation respectively.

It is hereby sent forth in the Name of God the Father, the Son, and the Holy Spirit; to equip the reader to "war" in prayer, and achieve much more than we can ever think or ask; I pray in the Name of Jesus Christ, Amen. Our God reigns! Maranatha!

Tofunmi Akinyemi (Mama Jochebed)
The KING's Throne Room.
Thursday, August 24, 2017.

1
Daddy's Direct Line

Introduction

Prayer is Daddy's Direct Line (DDL); the channel through which Christians communicate with the Almighty God, our loving Heavenly Father. What a great privilege to have the direct line of the King of all the earth!

"For God is the King of all the earth... God reigns over the nations; God sits on His holy throne." Psalm 47:7 & 8.

God as our Father

When a person gets born again, one becomes a child of God; courtesy Jesus Christ.

"... as many as received Him, to them He gave the right to become children of God, to those who believe on His name." John 1:12.

It is also written: *"The Spirit Himself bears witness with our spirit that we are children of God."* Romans 8:16.

God's Princes and Princesses!

As it has been mentioned above, the Almighty God is the King of all the earth, and Christians are God's children. Therefore, Christians are Princes and Princesses of the King of kings!

Yes, Christians are members of God's Royal Family; whatever may be one's status in life. The Bible says: *"... You are no longer strangers... but... members of the household of God..."* Ephesians 2:19.

This great privilege should gladden us, and make us eternally grateful to God. It should also challenge us to daily live holy, as worthy of Royalty; so that our lives will continually bring honour and glory to God.

God desires our fellowship

The Almighty God desires to continually interact with all His children throughout our earthly sojourn; to keep in touch with us until we safely get "Home". This is made possible through prayers.

"... you received the spirit of adoption by whom we cry out, Abba, Father." Romans 8:15.

In the manner in which we interact with a person we truly love, and we know truly loves us, Christians are expected to regularly go to God's Presence. We can be assured of His glad welcome.

The Royal Privilege

The Bible says: *"Because of Christ and our faith in Him, we can now come boldly and confidently into God's presence."* Ephesians 3:12 (NLT).

It is a great privilege to have access to the Royal Presence of His Majesty, the King of all the earth! We must not take this for granted, but jealously guard over it.

Therefore, for unhindered access to God our Father, we must daily live in obedience to Him all our days; because God is: *"... of purer eyes than to behold evil, and cannot look on wickedness...."* Habakkuk 1:13a.

The Christian and Prayer

The Almighty God says: *"Call to Me, and I will answer you, and show you great and mighty things, which you do not know."* (Jeremiah 33:3). This is an assurance that God will answer us when we call on Him.

"Let us therefore come boldly to the throne of grace, that we may obtain mercy and find grace to help in time of need." Hebrews 4:16.

Please Note: As we come to God in prayers, we must not come empty-handed; we are to come with praise, worship and thanksgiving. It is written: *"Enter into His gates with thanksgiving, and into His courts with praise. Be thankful to Him, and bless His name."* Psalm 100:4.

The Name of Jesus Christ

Christians are to pray to God in the Name of Jesus Christ. It is the only valid "Signature" to the "cheque" of our prayer requests from the "Throne Room Bank".

Jesus says: *"... most assuredly, I say to you, whatever you ask the Father in My name He will give you."* John 16:23.

Also, the Name of Jesus Christ is above all other names, and it is the most excellent Name. The power of Jesus' Name is effective in all realms – heaven, earth, and under the earth. The Bible says:

"... God also has highly exalted Him and given Him the name which is above every name, that at the name of Jesus every knee should bow, of those in heaven, and of those on earth, and of those under the earth, and that every tongue should confess that Jesus Christ is Lord, to the glory of God the Father." Philippians 2:9-11.

Our God is unequalled!

Our God has no equal, and He is Almighty. He has the power to help us, and He is the only One who can help us. He can be trusted with our challenges and worries. God says of Himself:

"To whom will you liken Me, and make me equal and compare Me, that we should be alike?... For I am God, and there is no other; I am God, and there is none like Me...." Isaiah 46:5 & 9.

God cares about you

As you run the race Home, always remember that you have a very powerful and loving Heavenly Father. He cares very much about you, and is ever willing to help you as you "cry" unto Him in the beauty of holiness.

"As a father pities his children, so the Lord pities those who fear Him." Psalm 103:13.

Call upon God

In view of all the above, is anything troubling you; or is there any challenge you are facing? "DDL" it to God Almighty; that is, "Daddy-Direct-Line" it to God Almighty via prayer. The Bible says:

"Be anxious for nothing, but in everything by prayer and supplication, with thanksgiving, let your requests be made known to God; and the peace of God, which

surpasses all understanding, will guard your hearts and minds through Christ Jesus." Philippians 4:5 & 6.

Perhaps...

- You have just received a letter in the post, and it contains a negative news; or is it a negative report from your Doctor? You are out of job; or is it about your Immigration Status in a foreign land?

- Your house is about to be taken over because you have defaulted in paying the mortgage or rent? You are facing challenges in your child-rearing, marriage, ministerial calling; or in your work?

- You have been praying for the salvation of souls; for personal, or corporate revival?

- You have been waiting on God for the fruit of the womb? You have been trusting God for a life-partner, that plum job, or contract award? The list is endless!

Do not despair; instead, confidently go before God in prayers; tell Him about your challenges, needs, fears, and concerns. He knows them, but He wants you to talk to Him about it all. Ask Him to help you; and He sure will.

The Help of the Holy Spirit

As mere mortals, there are times we feel overwhelmed by what we go through in the wilderness of this world. Therefore, we may feel weary in the place of prayers, our communication channel with God; who is our only Source of Help.

At such times, when we are too weary to pray, or don't even know what to pray for; the Holy Spirit helps us, and prays through us according to God's will.

"Likewise the Spirit also helps in our weaknesses. For we do not know what we should pray for as we ought, but the Spirit Himself makes intercession for us with groanings which cannot be uttered... He makes intercession for the saints according to the will of God." Romans 8:26 & 27.

Conclusion

Communication is a two-way thing. Therefore, as we present our requests to God, it is wise to be attentive to hear whatever God may want to tell us - a sense of direction in prayers, insight to situations, encouragement, His loving rebuke etc.

As we regularly appear before God, and are soaked in His Presence, His Glory rubs on us. This empowers us for holy living, and also equips us to make positive impact in our generation.

2
Persist in Prayers

Jesus' Parable on Prayer

Our Lord Jesus Christ often spoke in parables during His earthly Ministry. He did this to teach the lessons of the Kingdom, one of such parables was on the need to be persistent in prayers.

"Then He spoke a parable to them, that men always ought to pray and not loose heart, saying: "There was in a certain city a judge who did not fear God nor regard man.

Now there was a widow in that city; and she came to him, saying, Get justice for me from my adversary; and he would not for a while; but afterward he said within himself, "Though I do not fear God nor regard man, yet because this widow troubles me I will avenge her, lest by her continual coming she weary me."

Then the Lord said, "Hear what the unjust judge said. And shall God not avenge His own elect who cry out day and night to Him, though He bears long with them? I tell you He will avenge them speedily...." Luke 18:1-8a.

Persist in Prayer

The above parable from the very mouth of our Lord Jesus Christ shows that persistent praying is very important to the Christian on life's path. He admonished us to persist in prayers against all odds.

Jesus Christ knew there are circumstances that will attempt to discourage us from persistent praying, especially when the physical manifestation of our requests seems not to be quickly forthcoming.

However, we are to be persistent like the Luke 18 woman who refused to give up on her request, despite being spitefully treated by the ungodly Judge.

The widow's persistence made the Judge to grant the widow's request; even though for his own selfish reason (to get the widow off his back); and not because he cared about the widow's plight! This ungodly Judge said:

"... Though I do not fear God nor regard man, yet because this widow troubles me I will avenge her, lest by her

continual coming she weary me." Luke 18:4 & 5.

Our Merciful God

If the ungodly Judge granted the widow's request because of the latter's persistence, how much more will our <u>loving</u> Heavenly Father answer the prayers of His children?

"... And shall God not avenge His own elect who cry out day and night to Him, though He bears long with them? I tell you He will avenge them speedily...." Luke 18:6-8a.

This should encourage our hearts to be prayerful. The One we are praying to is unlike the ungodly Judge; rather, He is our very caring and merciful God!

Please Note: It is very important that our prayers are not centred on material acquisitions alone. *"... for one's life does not consist in the abundance of the things he possesses."* Luke 12:15.

Therefore, Christians should always remember to pray for personal spiritual growth, for the salvation of souls; for spiritual revival in the Body of Christ etc.

Keep applying the 'Fire'

In the light of all the above, be courageous and do not stop praying; neither waver in your faith in God.

"So Jesus answered and said to them, "Assuredly, I say to you, if you have faith and do not doubt, you will not

only do what was done to the fig tree, but also if you say to this mountain, 'Be removed and be cast into the sea,' it will be done." Matthew 21:21.

Therefore, refuse to be discouraged; keep trusting, and patiently wait for God. The Almighty God will surely arise to help you in the nick of time.

Keep applying the "fire" of prayers to your needs and challenges, and in your intercession for others. A time will come when your challenges will "melt", and give way under the pressure of prayer fire!

Conclusion

Do not give up praying, and do not give up on God. Always remember that *"... men always ought to pray and not loose heart...."* Luke 18:1.

3

Be an Intercessor

Introduction

As Christians pray without ceasing, we are expected to also pray for others. Our prayers should not only be for ourselves, and our loved ones; we are to pray for individuals, the Church, the society, and the nations. The Bible says:

"Therefore, I exhort first of all that supplications, prayers, intercessions, and giving of thanks be made for all men, for kings and all who are in authority, that we

may lead a quiet and peaceable life in all godliness and reverence." 1 Timothy 2:1 & 2.

The Christian and Intercession

In view of the above, Christians are expected to couple our prayers with thanksgiving to God, and also remember to pray for all; for the unsaved, the lonely, the sick, the rich, the poor, those who are hurting; those in government and positions of authority - whether in the family, Church, Schools etc.

"For this is good and acceptable in the sight of God our Saviour, who desires all men to be saved and to come to the knowledge of the truth." 1 Timothy 2:3 & 4.

Standing in the Gap

There are times that Christians are genuinely concerned about the failures of fellow brethren; that of Church leaders, the moral decadence in the society, and in the nations of the world.

However, we must note that merely showing concern, or talking about the ills will not produce any solution. Yes, talking helps no one; but praying about it all will be beneficial to all.

Therefore, rather than just talk, we are expected to stand in the gap through intercessory praying, and sharing the Goodnews of salvation through Jesus Christ.

Also, Christians are to uphold one another in prayers. Thus we can be strengthened to forge ahead in the Christian race, finish strong, and make heaven at last.

When we pray for others, including the rulers and spiritual leaders, we are indirectly praying for ourselves. This is because when the society is peaceful, and its people are godly, then we shall live in peace.

Intercession is good

The Bible says that intercession is good and acceptable in God's sight (1 Timothy 2:3). This means that failure to interecede is bad, and unacceptable in God's sight. Therefore, Christians should be fervently involved in the Ministry of intercession.

Intercession and Evangelism

If Christians will succeed in fulfilling "The "Great Commission" of Evangelism and discipleship (Matthew 28:18-20), a regular fervent intercession for the unsaved is non-negotiable.

We must be ready to "war" for the souls of the unsaved; that the Almighty God will "open" the eyes of their understanding about God's plan of salvation through Jesus Christ.

This is because the Gospel "... *is veiled to those who are perishing, whose minds the god of this age has blinded... lest the light of the gospel of the glory of Christ, who is the image of God, should shine on them."* 2 Corinthians 4:4.

As we fervently intercede for the unsaved, God will touch their hearts, and make them receptive to the Gospel. This is the secret of true and lasting Church growth.

It is equally important to disciple and pray for our converts to stand for Christ. We are to intercede for backsliders too; rather than talk about them, or look down on them.

Benefits of Intercession

Intercession is highly beneficial to the intercessor, and to all men; and some of these benefits are:

- **It attracts God's blessing to us.**

As earlier mentioned, intercession is pleasing unto God. When we do God's pleasure, He will be happy with us, and will surely bless us.

- **More souls will be "harvested" into God's Kingdom.**

When Christians intercede for the unsaved, God will surely touch their hearts, and save their souls; because God *"... desires all men to be saved and to come to the knowledge of the truth."* 1 Timothy 2:4.

This way, more people will be able to enjoy the abundant life made available through Jesus Christ

(John 10:10b). As they are discipled for Christ, they will stand, and go out to win others for Jesus Christ.

- **We become more prayerful**

You spend more time in the prayer closet more than you would have done if you are only praying for yourself and your loved ones. This sharpens your prayer life.

- **Empowerment for the race**

As we tarry in God's awesome Presence, we are renewed in grace for the Christian race.

- **A closer walk with God**

The time we spend in the prayer closet enriches our intimacy with God. This increases our knowledge of God, and grants us a closer walk with Him. We are also strengthened to win and disciple more souls for Christ.

- **A peaceful Life**

Our intimacy with God puts our mind at rest in Him. This helps us to have inner peace inspite of the perilous times we are living in.

- **A better Society**

The spiritual controls the physical. Therefore, praying for the society and its rulers may be expected to produce good governance, and also a relatively peaceful society than we would have had without intercession.

- **Great Rewards from God**

The Almighty God will reward the Christian intercessor; both in this world, and in eternity. *"For God is not unjust to forget your work and labour of love...."* Hebrews 6:10.

Conclusion

As earlier mentioned, intercessory praying is good and acceptable before God; therefore, Christians ought to embrace it for our own good, that of the Kingdom, and the society at large.

4
Be Rich in God's Word

The Word of God is the Lifeline for Christians in the wilderness of this world. It is not surprising therefore that the Bible says:

"Let the Word of Christ dwell in you richly in all wisdom, teaching and admonishing one another in psalms and hymns and spiritual songs, singing with grace in your hearts to the Lord." Colossians 3:16.

As Christians, we are expected to constantly fill our hearts with God's Word; allowing it to mould us, and believing that it will do what God says it will do! A heart-knowledge (not just a head-knowledge) of God's Word makes it effective in our lives and situations.

God's Word in the heart

The Word of God in your heart:

- **Sharpens your faith in God**

"So then faith comes by hearing, and hearing by the word of God." (Romans 10:17). This sets you up to pray through, and receive your miracles from God.

- **Keeps you away from sin!**

The Word of God guides you on the path of holiness. *"Your Word is a lamp to my feet and a light to my path."* Psalm 119:105.

It also helps you to live holy, thereby preserving you in the Christian race.*"Your word I have hidden in my heart, that I might not sin against You."* Psalm 119:11.

In view of the above, sin which is the major hindrance to answered prayers is removed, because the Bible says: *"If I regard iniquity in my heart, the Lord will not hear."* Psalm 66:18.

- **Increases your knowledge of God**

The more you know God, the more you are able to trust Him. Also, you are strengthened in prayers, and every aspect of your life. *"... the people who know their God shall be strong, and carry out great exploits."* Daniel 11:32b.

- **Gives a faith-filled mind-set**

You have a healthy mindset that God is able to do all things This enables you to confidently present your prayer requests to God, believing that you will receive answers to them. *"For with God nothing will be impossible."* Luke 1:37.

- **Gives God's peace**

 A heart full of God's Word will be full of God's peace! There will be no room for anxiety, depression and fear; even in the midst of the storms!

 "... The peace of God, which surpasses all understanding, will guard your hearts and minds through Christ Jesus." Philippians 4:7.

- **Fires you up to pray**

As above-mentioned, your word level increases your faith level (Romans 10:17); and an increased faith in God births increased prayer fire.

- **Helps you to pray aright**

God's Word in your heart helps you to live holy, and gives you a closer walk with God. You are able to know the mind of God, and thereby pray in alignment with His will. *"The secret of the Lord is with those who fear Him...."* Psalm 25: 14.

- **Brings Answers to prayers**

The Word of God helps you to know God's Mind, how to pray, and what to pray about. When you pray according to the will of God, you receive answers to your prayers.

"Now this is the confidence that we have in Him, that if we ask anything according to His will, He hears us." 1 John 5:14.

Conclusion

In view of all the above, a heart knowledge of God's Word is indeed a boost to the Christian's prayer life; and also, the Lifeline in the wilderness of this world.

5
Be God's Word Compliant

Introduction

It is worthy of note that embracing God's plan of salvation for mankind is the first necessary step to being God's Word compliant.

Before you can have the power to live according to God's Word, you must have genuinely repented from sins, and accepted Jesus Christ as your personal Lord and Saviour.

Are you Saved?

If yes, glory to God! Please, continue to live for Jesus Christ till the end of your life, and ensure that you are actively taking part in Evangelism and Discipleship.

However, if you are not born again, this is too great a risk; both in this world and eternity. Therefore, repent and give your life to Jesus Christ <u>now</u> before it is too late; you don't know when it may be too late, so don't delay.

The Christian and obedience to God

The Christian (a person who is genuinely born again) has been called to a life of total obedience to the Word of God; as contained in the Holy Bible.

Obedience to God is honouring to Him; and also the acid test of our love for Him. Our Lord Jesus Christ says: *"If you love Me, keep My commandments."* John 14:15.

Obedience attracts persecutions!

When you live in obedience to God, you will surely be persecuted! Always remember this, so that you will not be discouraged when persecutions come.

"Yes, and all who desire to live godly in Christ Jesus will suffer persecution." 2 Timothy 3:12.

Obedience and prayers

The Christian's obedience to God is a major condition to receiving answers to prayers. The Bible says: *"If I regard iniquity in my heart, the Lord will not hear."* Psalm 66:18.

Therefore, as Christians come before God in prayers (individually or corporately), the issue of sin must first be settled. This is not only to receive answers to prayers; but more so, because of one's eternal welfare.

Evangelism and Prayers

Christians who win and disciple souls for Christ are obeying God as per "The Great Commission" (Matthew 28:18-20). Active involvement in Evangelism and Discipleship opens the door to answered prayers for the Christian. Jesus Christ says:

"You did not choose Me; but I chose you and appointed you that you should go and bear fruit and that your fruit should abide, so that whatever you ask the Father in My name, He may give it you." John 15:16.

Evangelism and Discipleship bring pleasure to God; so Christians who are actively involved in them have a "hot line" to God, and will receive answers to their prayers.

"And whatever we ask we receive from Him, because we keep His commandments and do those things that are pleasing in His sight." 1 John 3:22.

This should encourage Christians to be actively involved in Evangelism and Discipleship; not only to have answered prayers, but mainly out of love to obey God, and because of our eternal welfare.

Some Benefits of Obedience

There are many benefits to be enjoyed by Christians who have a lifestyle of obedience to God; and some of these are:

- **God's special Treasure!**

"Now therefore, if you will indeed obey My voice and keep My covenant, then you shall be a special treasure to Me above all people; for all the earth is Mine." Exodus 19:5.

It is a great privilege to be God's special treasure; you will have access to special privileges from the King of kings.

- **Unhindered access to God**

Living victoriously over sin removes the barrier between you and God. When the "blockage" of sin is removed, we have a sure access to God's Royal Presence; to have an audience with Him.

"... the Lord's hand is not shortened, that it cannot save; nor His ear heavy, that It cannot hear. But your iniquities have separated you from God; and your sins have hidden His face from you, so that He will not hear." Isaiah 59:1 & 2.

- **God's attentiveness to our prayers.**

As mentioned in Isaiah 59:1 & 2 above, sin hides God's face from you; such that He will not hear you when you pray. However, when the issue of sin is dealt with, the Lord will be attentive to one's prayers.

- **Praying with the right motive.**

A holy lifestyle will enable you to pray with the right motive; which is, to glorify God. This removes a major hinderance to prayers because the Bible says:

"You ask and do not receive, because you ask amiss, that you may spend it on your pleasures." James 4:3.

When your motive for praying is pure, and not for self-aggrandisement; this sets you up for receiving from God.

- **Answered Prayers**

When you live to please God, and your prayers align with His will, you receive the physical manifestation of your requests from God; more so that you are God's special Treasure!

"And whatever we ask we receive from Him, because we keep His commandments and do those things that are pleasing in His sight." 1 John 3:22.

- **You become Jesus' friend**

Our Lord Jesus Christ says: *"You are My friends if you do whatever I command you."* John 15:14.

This means that an obedient Christian is a friend of Jesus Christ. As Jesus' friend, you have access to special privileges, and "classified information" from God; courtesy Jesus Christ, the Son of the King of kings.

As an obedient Christian, be assured that you are greatly cherished by God above all others that *"... he who touches you touches the apple of His eye."* Zechariah 2:8b.

Also, your privileged position as Jesus' friend gives you access to privileged insights, guidance, revelations etc. It is written: *"The secret of the Lord is with those who fear Him...."* Psalm 25: 14.

- **Wisdom to pray aright**

Your privileged position helps you to know the mind of God. This guides you to know what to ask God in prayer; thus enabling you to pray in line with God's will.

- **Impactful Prayer Life**

The prayers of the obedient Christian becomes very powerful and effective; both in one's life and generation. *"... The effective, fervent prayer of a righteous man avails much."* James 5:16b.

- **Peace and joy**

A life of obedience to God gives you peace and joy *"For the kingdom of God is ... righteousness and peace and joy in the Holy Spirit."* Romans 14:17.

- **God's blessings**

Obedience to God attracts His blessings to you and your generations.

"... the mercy of the Lord is from everlasting to everlasting on those who fear Him, and His righteousness to children's children, to such as keep His covenant, and to those who remember His commandments to do them." Psalm 103:17 & 18.

- **Heaven at Last!**

When you live in obedience to God till the end; apart from receiving answers to your prayers, you will be preserved in the Christian race and will make heaven at last. Heaven is for only those who do God's will.

"Not everyone who says to Me, Lord, Lord, shall enter the kingdom of heaven, but he who does the will of My Father in heaven." Matthew 7:21.

Conclusion

As earlier mentioned in this Chapter, if you are not yet saved, repent now, before it is too late! (See Chapter Twenty-seven for details). Then live in obedience to God till the end of your life; this will guarantee your eternal rest with God.

6
Refuse all Negative Emotions

Introduction

"Negative emotions can be described as any feeling which causes you to be miserable and sad. These emotions make you dislike yourself and others, and take away your confidence; emotions like hate, anger, jealousy and sadness...

Negative emotions can dampen our enthusiasm for life, depending on how long we let them affect us....

Negative emotions stop us from thinking and behaving rationally and seeing situations in their true perspective... and prevents us from enjoying life." Source: Better Health Channel www.betterhealth.vic.gov.au

The reality of Negative Emotions

Negative emotions are real. When people feel overwhelmed by the challenges of life, they may resort to any of the following negative emotions.

Self-pity, sorrow, anxiety, fear, doubt, anger, hatred, envy, resentment, bitterness, unforgiveness, guilt, regret, shame, self-hatred, depression, aloneness; feeling helpless and hopeless etc.

Negative Emotions are destructive

Negative emotions do not solve any problem, but rather create more for you. They are physically, emotionally and spiritually destructive; slowly and silently "killing" its victim! They are capable of:

- Sapping your physical energy.

- Draining you emotionally.

- Causing diseases like hypertension, stroke, cancer etc.

- Robbing you of God's peace and joy.

- Defiling and weighing you down; thereby drawing one back in the Christian race.

The Christian and Challenges

As you run the race Home, you will surely encounter moments of challenges. Our Lord Jesus Christ gave this hint in His Valedictory Words to His disciples; however, He encouraged Christians to be of good cheer, because He has overcome for us.

"These things I have spoken to you, that in Me you may have peace. In the world you will have tribulation; but be of good cheer, I have overcome the world." John 16:33.

Our Burden Bearer

The Almighty God did not "design" you to carry your burdens by yourself; rather, you are to take your challenges to God in prayers. The Bible says: *"Casting all your care upon Him, for He cares for you."* 1 Peter 5:7.

When you fail to cast your cares upon the Lord, but try to carry them in your own strength, you will be weighed down; and become an easy "prey" to any of the above-mentioned negative emotions.

This steals your faith in God, weakens you in the place of prayers; and causes the fire on your Prayer Altar to <u>gradually</u> go down! It also makes you feel helpless and hopeless!

The feeling of hopelessness in the life of a Christian is an insult on the Almighty God, as if He is unable to help; whereas, *"God is our refuge and strength, a very present help in trouble."* Psalm 46:1.

It is therefore very important for you to be deliberate about <u>regularly</u> casting your cares upon the Lord; otherwise, you become a casualty on life's battle-field!

Negative Emotions and Prayers

Negative emotions are not prayer-friendly! They defile you, and also hinder your prayers e.g. unforgiveness. The Bible says:

"And whenever you stand praying, if you have anything against anyone, forgive him, that your Father in heaven may also forgive you your trespasses. But if you do not forgive, neither will your Father in heaven forgive your trespasses." Mark 11:25 & 26.

When you cannot receive forgiveness for your sins, this is a sure blockage to prayers!

Say No to Negative Emotions

Any of the above negative emotions will attempt to "invade" your life; but disallow them. Yes, reject all forms of negative emotions; and thereby be free from its damaging effects.

Therefore, refuse all negative emotions; don't approve of them, don't be pleased with them, don't give in to them, prevent them from settling down in your life!

The Bible's wise counsel is for Christians to "... *lay aside every weight, and the sin which so easily ensnares us....*" Hebrews 1:1b.

Power through Christ

By your own power, you cannot resist the "trap" of negative emotions. However, you can have victory through Christ; as you depend on the indwelling Holy Spirit. *"I can do all things through Christ who strengthens me."* Philippians 4:13.

Refusing Negative Emotions

When you refuse to succumb to any form of negative emotions:

- You are relieved of "weights" that would have slowed you down; or get you grounded in the Christian race.

- You are protected against diseases caused by negative emotions; thereby being physically enabled to persist in prayers.

- You will be emotionally balanced; thus, you can think straight, and pray aright.

- You are spiritually healthy and enabled to maintain a steady growth in Christ. This makes your prayers effective.

- Your spiritual antenna is sharpened to receive from God e.g. inspirations, revelations, encouragements, sense of directions; how to pray, and what to pray for etc.

- The joy of the Lord fills your heart, and this strengthens you in the inner man to tarry in the place of prayers; because, "... *the joy of the Lord is your strength."* Nehemiah 8:10b.

- You are preserved on the path of holiness, and your prayers become very effective.

- You are enabled to fulfil God's purpose for your life.

- As you live holy to the end, you make heaven at last.

Conclusion

As a Christian, if you have been caught in any form of negative emotion, please, <u>urgently</u> repent, and run to the Almighty God for help.

Repent, and ask for God's forgiveness, after which you rededicate your life to Jesus Christ. This opens you to God's healing, and the perfection of all that concerns you.

My beloved reader, perhaps you are not yet born again, urgently repent from sin, and receive Jesus Christ as your personal Lord and Saviour. GOD BLESS.

7
Embrace a Fasted Lifestyle

Introduction

We cannot talk of a fasted lifestyle without first discussing what fasting is. Fasting is abstaining from food, and this can be observed individually or corporately. It is a spiritual exercise which yields both physical and spiritual benefits.

This is very Important

The Bible says, *"... wisdom is profitable to direct."* Ecclesiastes 10:10b (KJV).

In as much as fasting is beneficial, it is very important to note that fasting may not be recommended for expectant mothers!

Those with health challenges should consult their Doctors before embarking on any form of fast. This is to ensure they don't engage in what will be detrimental to their health. Even healthy people ought to fast informedly to remain healthy!

Also, when lawfully married couples accompany their fastings with sexual abstinence, the Bible expects it to be by mutual consent, and should not be prolonged. The Bible says:

"Do not deprive one another except with consent for a time, that you may give yourselves to fasting and prayer; and come together again so that satan does not tempt you because of your lack of self-control." 1 Corinthians 7:5.

The Aims of Fasting

The main aim of fasting is to set time apart, to nurture your intimacy with God; through prayers, praises, and the study of the Bible. This may mean reduction of the time spent on other things like leisure, or browsing the social media etc.

Some of the other aims of fasting include:

- To regulate your appetite and desires; so that you are not enslaved by fleshly indulgencies.

- To discipline the flesh, so that it can be under the control of the Spirit; this is for your all-round benefit.

- To humble your soul before God, in order to seek His help and guidance. This can be done individually, at family levels, and corporately as a Church, or nation.

- To prepare for spiritual warfare.

This could be to battle for the souls of men; for genuine conversions and salvation. It could also be to break the yokes of sin, addictions, or afflictions; whether in your life, or those of others; or in the Church, or over a nation.

- To seek God's face in repentance.

Fasting can be for personal, congregational, or national repentance. For example, Daniel prayed and fasted for the nation of Israel.

"Then I set my face toward the Lord God to make request by prayer and supplications, with fasting... And I prayed to the Lord my God, and made confession, and said... we have sinned and committed iniquity, we have done wickedly and rebelled... O my God, incline Your ear and hear; open your eyes and see our desolations... because of your great mercies. O Lord, hear! O Lord, forgive! ...." Daniel 9:3-19.

In the manner in which Daniel prayed about national repentance, the Christian can do so for personal or family repentance; so also the Church for corporate repentance.

What Fasting is not

1. It is not Salvation

Fasting is not to punish yourself for your sins in order to be saved. Salvation is not through works; but rather by grace, and faith in Jesus Christ's atonement for the sins of the world.

"For by grace you have been saved through faith, and that not of yourselves; it is the gift of God, not of works, lest anyone should boast." Ephesians 2:8.

Please note: Mankind can only be saved through genuine repentance and forsaking of sins; and accepting Jesus Christ as personal Lord and Saviour. The Bible says:

"The sacrifices of God are a broken spirit, a broken and a contrite heart – these, O God, You will not despise." Psalm 51:17.

2. It is not synonymous with holiness

Fasting is not what makes the Christian holy, but living in obedience to God till the end of one's life. *"... Behold, to obey is better than sacrifice...."* 1 Samuel 15:22b.

3. It is not for formality

Fasting is to be observed with a purpose, and <u>not</u> just as a religious ritual. It is to be coupled with a heart burdened for prayer. For example, when Ezra was leading the exiles back to Jerusalem, he led the people to fast and pray for God's guidance, and protection on the journey.

"Then I proclaimed a fast... that we might humble ourselves before our God, to seek from Him the right way for us and our little ones and all our posessions." Ezra 8:21.

4. It is not bribery

Fasting is not to bribe God to bless us. It is your spiritual commitment to concentrate on your prayer requests from God; an outer sign of your earnest inner desire for help.

5. It is not for self-aggrandizement

Fasting is not to glorify self, but rather to glorify God. *"Therefore, whether you eat or drink, or whatever you do, do all to the glory of God."* 1 Corinthians 10:31.

6. It is not for show-off

You are not to fast to be seen of men; perhaps, to show how spiritual you are. The Bible says:

"... when you fast, do not be like the hypocrites, with a sad countenance. For they disfigure their faces that they may appear to men to be fasting. Assuredly, I say to you, they have their reward.

But you, when you fast, anoint your head and wash your face, so that you do not appear to men to be fasting, but to your Father who is in secret place; and your Father who sees in secret will reward you openly." Matthew 6: 16-18.

7. It is not for weight loss

Effective fasting is not aimed at loosing weight; that will be dieting! As earlier mentioned, fasting is to set time apart for prayers, praises and the study of the Word; so as to nurture your intimacy with God.

Fasting and Prayers

Fasting is an essential part of effective praying; whether concerning your personal prayer requests, intercessory praying for individuals, nations, or the Church of God.

This is because there are some "mountains" that need the combination of both prayer and fasting to move them. *"However, this kind does not go out except by prayer and fasting."* Matthew 17:21.

An example was when King Jehoshaphat was threatened by the people of Ammon, Moab, and Mount Seir. He sought God's help in prayer by declaring a corporate fast, coupled with high level praise!

"And Jehoshaphat feared, and set himself to seek the Lord, and proclaimed a fast throughout all Judah. So

Judah gathered together to ask help from the Lord; and from all the cities of Judah they came to seek the Lord.

... Now all Judah, with their little ones, their wives, and their children, stood before the Lord.... Now when they began to sing and to praise, the Lord set ambushes against the people of Ammon, Moab, and Mount Seir, who had come against Judah; and they were defeated." 2 Chronicles 20:3,4,13 & 22.

In response to their corporate prayer and fasting, the Almighty God set the stage for the defeat of the enemies of Israel. God can do the same for individuals, families, Churches or nations.

Effective Fasting and Praying

As you pray and fast, there are steps to be taken to make them effective; some of these are:

- **A life of obedience to God**

A life of obedience to God is necessary for effective fasting. The Bible says:

"Has the Lord as great delight in burnt offerings and sacrifices, as in obeying the voice of the Lord? Behold, to obey is better than sacrifice...." 1 Samuel 15:22.

- **Dealing kindly with others**

The Almighty God expects you to show kindness, fairness, and forgiveness in your interactions with others; and to also give to the less-privileged. God says:

"Is this not the fast that I have chosen: to loose the bonds of wickedness, to undo the heavy burdens, to let the oppressed go free, and that you break every yoke?

Is it not to share your bread with the hungry, and that you bring to your house the poor who are cast out; when you see the naked, that you cover him, and not hide yourself from your own flesh?" Isaiah 58:6 & 7.

Giving to the poor may be seen as a sort of fasting (or sacrificing) part of your personal belongings to provide for the needy. God will reward you for this. The Bible says:

"He who has pity on the poor lends to the Lord, and He will pay back what he has given." Proverbs 19:17.

- **Living a disciplined life**

Living a disciplined life is to embrace moderation in all things. This tames the flesh in its insatiable and spiritually deadly cravings! The Bible's admonition to you is: *"Let your moderation be known unto all men. The Lord is at hand."* Philippians 4:5.

You are to be disciplined in your appetite for food and material acquisitions. Thus, you have more to sacrifice for the needy, the Ministers of God, and the spread of the Gospel etc.

You are to avoid greed for food, material things, and all forms of self-indulgences. *"... Take heed and beware of covetousness, for one's life does not consist in the abundance of the things he possesses."* Luke 12:15.

When you are disciplined in your desires, you will be shielded from fulfilling "the lust of the flesh, the lust of the eyes", and from manifesting "the pride of life" (1 John 2:16). This equips you for effective fasting and praying.

A fasted lifestyle

A fasted lifestyle is used here to mean that the Christian is to regularly fast. Please, be reminded that this should be done informedly, so that you don't put your health at risk.

A fasted lifestyle has been used here to include:

- Being disciplined about eating, even when you are not fasting. This gives you a preparedness to fast on short notice from the Holy Spirit; a sort of spiritual battle-readiness at all times!

- Showing moderation in the acquisition of material things, and in the use of other legitimate things like sleep, internet, sex (for the lawfully married) etc.

- Self-control in talking and behaviour.

Examples from the Bible

There are examples of people in the Bible who had a fasted lifestyle, and impacted their generations for God. Some of these are:

1. **Nehemiah**

Nehemiah was one of the Israelites taken captive to Babylon. When he heard that Jerusalem (his fatherland), and its inhabitants were in a very bad condition, he fasted and prayed for many days.

"So it was, when I heard these words, that I sat down and wept, and mourned for many days; I was fasting and praying before the God of heaven." Nehemiah 1:4.

2.   Prophetess Anna

She was a widow who served God with a fasted lifestyle.

"Now there was... Anna, a Prophetess... a widow of about eighty-four years, who did not depart from the temple, but served God with fastings and prayers night and day." Luke 2:36 & 37.

3.   The Apostles

The Apostles often fasted. Paul said *"... in all things we commend ourselves as ministers of God: in much patience, in tribulations, in needs, in distresses... in fastings; by purity...."* 2 Corinthians 6:3-6.

The Apostle Paul often fasted as he fulfilled his Ministry:

"... in stripes, above measure, in prisons more frequently... in weariness and toil, in sleeplessness often, in hunger and thirst, in fastings often, in cold and nakedness...." 2 Corinthians 11:22-33.

Benefits of a fasted Lifestyle

There are many benefits you enjoy when you couple your prayers with fasting, and some of these are:

- **Your flesh is subdued**

A fasted lifestyle helps you to limit the flesh in its carnal desires and appetites. This subdues your flesh to the control of the Holy Spirit, helps you to live holy; thereby strengthening you in the place of prayers.

- **A closer walk with God**

As you consistently spend time in the prayer closet, you have an increasing bond with God, and this boosts your spiritual growth.

- **Anointing for Exploits**

Time spent in God's Presence exposes you to His glory and anointing. The anointing breaks yokes, empowers you for holy living, and to pray more; also to do great exploits for God.

- **A sensitive spiritual antenna**

Your spiritual antennae is sharpened, and you are enabled to keenly receive "spiritual signals" from God's Throne Room - wisdom, insight, guidance, and inspiration through God's Holy Spirit. For example, the Apostles of old received guidance as they fasted and prayed.

"As they ministered to the Lord and fasted, the Holy Spirit said, now separate to Me Barnabas and Saul for the work to which I have called them. Then having fasted

and prayed, and laid hands on them, they sent them away." Acts 13:2 & 3.

- **A vibrant prayer life.**

A closer intimacy with God will increase your thirst for more of His Presence, and this increasingly drives you to the prayer closet. This helps you to mature in your prayer life, and makes your prayers more effective.

- **God's Attention**

As you embark on the Biblical fasting discussed above, the Almighty God will be attentive to you, and respond to your cries.

"Then your light shall break forth like the morning, your healing shall spring forth speedily, and your righteousness shall go before you; the glory of the Lord shall be your rear guard. Then you shall call, and the Lord will answer, you shall cry, and He will say, Here I am." Isaiah 58:8 & 9.

- **Answered Prayers**

You will receive answers to your prayers; just like when Ezra and the people humbled themselves in prayer and fasting before the Lord, to seek His guidance and protection.

"So we fasted and entreated our God for this, and He answered our prayers." Ezra 8:23.

- **Spiritual Revival**

When individual Christians are spiritually healthy, the Church (the Body of Christ) will be revived. We shall be strengthened to win more souls for Christ, and thereby impact our generation for God.

- **Good physical health**

Regular fasting helps to cleanse the body system from impurities. This boosts your physical health, and by extension your prayer life.

- **Heaven at last!**

As you live in obedience to God till the end, you will receive great rewards, and also gain eternal life.

Conclusion

As you embrace a fasted lifestyle, and pray in alignment with God's will, you receive answers to your prayers - the moving of your "mountains"; the breaking of the strongholds of sin, yokes, and addictions.

8
Keep Growing in Christ

Introduction

Salvation is the beginning of a life-long spiritual journey, with the ultimate goal of making heaven; growing daily in Christ is required to achieve this.

If you are not growing spiritually, you will be sliding back <u>gradually</u>; and your prayer life will suffer for it. The Christian race is such that you are either pressing on; or you are <u>gradually</u> sliding back!

Growing in Christ

In Chapter Five, Christians are admonished to be God's Word Compliant for effective praying. However, the Christian race is much more than receiving answers to prayers in this world; it is also to make heaven.

"For what will it profit a man if he gains the whole world, and looses his own soul?" Mark 8:36.

Therefore, as we persist in prayers, each of us must keep growing in Christ till the end of our earthly sojourn. It is not over until it is over; one must have a consistently Bible-compliant lifestyle till the end.

The Lifeline

The Holy Bible is our spiritual food to stay alive in the Christian race. There is no short-cut to victorious christian living outside the Word of God. It is written:

"Your word I have hidden in my heart, that I might not sin against you." (Psalm 119:11). This means that if we don't hide God's Word in our hearts, we will sin against Him; this will be a drawback in our Christian growth.

Therefore, for consistent spiritual growth, one must be continually armed with the Word of God; studying, meditating, and obeying it. The Bble says:

"This Book of the Law shall not depart from your mouth, but you shall meditate in it day and night, that you may observe to do according to all that is written in it. For

then you will make your way prosperous, and then you will have good successs." Joshua 1:8.

Spiritual growth and Prayers

When you are growing in Christ, you will be preserved on the path of holiness. This sharpens your prayer life, and makes your prayers very potent.

"... The effective, fervent prayer of a righteous man avails much." James 5:16b.

Please, be reminded that the ultimate goal of living holy is not only for answered prayers; but to make heaven at last.

Seek no Repose

In view of all the above, Christians must not seek repose in the race until we safely get "Home"! We are like athletes running a race, we must not stop until we reach "the finishing line"; otherwise one will be disqualified.

We must keep going for Christ, and keep growing in Christ; despite the inevitable challenges of the Christian race. Let us be encouraged that:

"... the sufferings of this present time are not worthy to be compared with the glory which shall be revealed in us." Romans 8:18.

Therefore, don't give up the faith because of trials, nor comfort; or for whatever reason. We must daily rely on the Holy Spirit's empowerment to see us through to the finishing line.

"Blessed is the man who endures temptation; for when he has been approved, he will receive the crown of life which the Lord has promised to those who love Him." James 1:12.

Conclusion

It is important for Christians to keep growing in Christ till the end; not only for answered prayers, but because of our eternal welfare. Therefore: *"... beware lest you... fall from your... steadfastness... but grow in grace and knowledge of our Lord and Saviour Jesus Christ. To Him be glory both now and forever. Amen."* 2 Peter 3:17 & 18.

9

The Spiritual Warfare

Introduction

Warfare has been defined as: "The activity of fighting a war, often including the weapons and methods that are used." (Cambridge Dictionary); also as "Military operations between enemies." (Merriam-Webster Dictionary).

The Christian is engaged in a continuous war with the devil and his demons. This war is real; however, it is a spiritual one.

"For we do not wrestle against flesh and blood, but against principalities, against powers, against the rulers

of the darkness of this age, against spiritual hosts of wickedness in the heavenly places." Ephesians 6:12.

The Warfare

When a person becomes born again, you become an enemy of the devil, and he is always looking for ways to bring one back into sin. That is, the ultimate goal of the warfare is for the souls of men.

The warfare is between two spiritual enemies; the Soldiers of Christ (the Christians) headed by Jesus Christ; and the wicked forces of darkness, headed by the devil.

Our fight being against spiritual beings makes the warfare a very dangerous one. We are not fighting against physical beings that can be seen with physical eyes; yet they exist, and are bent on our destruction!

"The thief does not come except to steal, and to kill, and to destroy. I have come that they may have life, and that they may have it more abundantly." John 10:10.

The devil fights Christians to derail us, and make one fall from the faith. This is because he wants Christians to loose heaven like him. *"But thanks be to God, who gives us the victory through our Lord Jesus Christ."* 1 Corinthians 15:57.

Prayer and Warfare

Prayer (being a component of the Christian race) is a spiritual war; just like the Christian race itself. The devil often uses wiles against Christians to disable one in the place of prayers.

Some of the devil's wiles against Christians are: apathy, laziness, ignorance, discouragement, doubts, over-sleeping, procrastination; spiritual lukewarmness and coldness etc.

For our survival in the Christian race, and to make it safely Home, we must fight on our knees; we either pray or perish! For victory on the spiritual battle-field, Christians must be consistently prayerful till we reach Home safely.

Victory through Christ

Jesus Christ is the Lamb (without blemish) that was slain to redeem mankind from sin. He rose on the third day to save all who truly repent from sin, and put their trust in Him as personal Lord and Saviour.

The death and resurrection of Jesus Christ brought a fatal defeat to the devil (and his demons), and gave victory to all who are truly born again.

"And you, being dead in your trespasses and the uncircumcision of your flesh, He has made alive together with Him, having forgiven you all your trespasses, having wiped out the handwriting of requirements that was against us, which was contrary

to us. And He has taken it out of the way, having nailed it to the cross. Having disarmed principalities and powers, He made a public spectacle of them, triumphing over them in it." Colossians 2:13-15.

Some implications for Christians:

- You have been made alive with Jesus Christ.

- All your sins have been forgiven.

- Everything contrary to you has been removed, and nailed to the Cross on which Jesus Christ died.

- Principalities and powers (that is, the devil and his demons) have been <u>disarmed</u>, <u>disgraced</u> and <u>defeated</u> for you.

- You are fighting against an already conquered enemy; courtesy Jesus Christ.

Therefore, as we war in prayers on our Homeward journey, it is important to always remember that we are in a battle that is already won for us.

The Victory of the Cross

The finished work of the Cross has given us victory over satan, the flesh, and the world. Ours is to continually enforce the victory of the cross against the devil and his demons; by putting them where they belong – the place of defeat!

The Blood of Jesus Christ

The Blood of Jesus Christ has atoned for our sins and thereby:

- Gives us constant access to the Holy of Holies.

This makes it possible for you to present your prayers, petitions, praises, worship and thanksgiving to God. You also have the opportunity to receive all of God's help, guidance, security, and grace from the "Throne Room Bank"!

"... Brethren, having boldness to enter the Holiest by the Blood of Jesus... let us draw near with a true heart in full assurance of faith...." Hebrews 10:19 & 22.

- Speaks positive things on your behalf – help, provision, protection, deliverance etc.

"... Jesus Christ the Mediator of the new covenant, and... the blood of sprinkling that speaks better things than that of Abel." Hebrews 12:24.

- Gives victory

The Blood of Jesus Christ serves as your "spiritual insurance cover" against the powers of darkness. It is the spiritual insurance they cannot disregard; neither can any problem of life.

"... the accuser of our brethren... has been cast down. And they overcame him by the blood of the Lamb and by the word of their testimony...." Revelation 12:10 & 11.

Please Hear This!

In the place of prayers, Christians have access to the help of the Holy Spirit, the Name of Jesus Christ, the Word of God as the Sword of the Spirit; also the power of praises, worship and thanksgiving.

We also have the "spiritual insurance cover" of the Blood of Jesus Christ, and the benefits of the devil's total defeat on the Cross.

However, unlike the Christian:

- The devil and his demons cannot, and do not have the Holy Spirit; so, they cannot access His help.

- They cannot use the Name of Jesus Christ; the most excellent Name.

- They cannot use the Sword of the Spirit; though the devil in his usual wiles, can misquote it to his own disadvantage. Yes, to his own disadvantage because God's Word is only effective when it proceeds from a life of holiness.

- They cannot, and will not offer praise, worship and thanksgiving to God; though in the end, they have no choice than bow to the Lordship of Jesus Christ!

- They cannot benefit from the victory of the Cross, and the "spiritual insurance cover" it provides for Christians. The insurance doesn't cover them; it is only for the redeemed.

Christians have the upper hand

Christians are fully equipped for spiritual warfare, whereas the devil is permanently stripped of all powers; remember, he only uses wiles. This gives an absolute advantage to Christians over the arch-enemy.

That is, Christians have an utmost upper hand in the spiritual warfare against the devil; if only we can live holy, and be steadfast in the place of prayers.

Conclusion

When Christians couple prayers with holiness, each of us will be positioned for victory in spiritual warfare – positive changes in our lives and those of our loved ones; also in the Church, and the larger society. You will make heaven at last if one stands for Christ to the end.

10
Be Spiritually Sensitive

Introduction

The word "sensitive" has been defined as "quick to detect or respond to slight changes, signals or influences." (Oxforddictionaries.com).

Therefore, spiritual sensitivity is used here to mean how keenly the Christian can receive "spiritual signals" from God; through the Holy Spirit. This is only possible as we maintain a consistent growth in Christ.

As Christians war in prayers, coupled with a fasted lifestyle, there is the need to be spiritually sensitive. This will benefit our prayer lives, and maximize the effectiveness of our prayers.

Good Spiritual Network

In the physical, when the network of a service provider is very good, the quality of the telephone call (video or audio) will be greatly enhanced, and vice versa.

When your Christian life is very healthy, it is comparable to having a good spiritual network. Your spiritual antenna will be keenly sensitive to receive spiritual signals from God.

Bad Spiritual Network

This is used here to mean that a Christian's spiritual antenna is unable to receive spiritual signals from God; whether in the place of prayers, or any other aspects of one's life. Such a Christian is like a ship without a compass, and in danger of getting lost!

Dangers of poor Spiritual Signals

As above-mentioned, it is dangerous to be unable to pick "spiritual signals" from God; and here are some of the dangers:

- Inability to hear the Holy Spirit in His guidance on prayers, and in other areas of your life.

That is, one will be spiritually deaf. This is the pathway to spiritual disaster!

- Leaning on your own understanding; this may sometimes make you pray differently from what you should pray for.

- Asking for what may be outside God's will for us, and thereby having unanswered Prayers. This is because if one asks anything that is not in accordance with God's will, He will not hear us (1 John 5:14).

- Frustration and discouragement.

When God refuses to hear one's prayers, it may lead to frustration, discouragement; or looking for alternative solutions. Please, be reminded that *"Their sorrows shall be multiplied who hasten after another god...."* Psalm 16:4.

- Praying for what will bring leanness to one's soul. *"And He gave them their request, but sent leanness into their soul."* Psalm 106:15.

- Inability to see an impending danger until it arrives and consumes you. May we not become casualties on the spiritual battle-field in Jesus Christ's Name, Amen.

The Christian and spiritual sensitivity

In view of the above, let your spiritual antenna be keenly sensitive to the Holy Spirit as you go before

God in prayers. This is only possible through consistent Christian growth.

Benefits of Spiritual Sensitivity

Spiritual sensitivity in the place of prayers is beneficial to you in many ways; and some of these are:

1. You to be guided to pray aright, and receive God's best through prayers.

2. You will be enabled to receive messages, instructions, and guidance from the Almighty God; so also directions on how to pray, and what to pray for.

3. You will be at rest in the waiting period before the miracle; as you are enabled to tap grace directly from His Presence.

4. The peace of God will fill your heart as you are enabled to know that all is well; also, you may have a glimpse of what God is doing behind the scene on your behalf.

5. You are able to receive warnings of an impending danger, and what to do to avert it.

As the saying goes, "knowledge is power". Having a foreknowledge of danger helps you pray to prevent it. This saves you from avoidable losses and heartaches.

Conclusion

It is very important for Christians to be spiritually sensitive in the place of prayers. This helps us to pray aright, saves us from avoidable calamities; and makes us victorious on the spiritual battle-field.

11
Your Mindset and You

Definition of keywords

The following words have been used here as follows:

1. **Mindset**

"A particular way of thinking: a person's attitude or set of opinions about something." (Merriamwebster.com)

"A habitual or characteristic mental attitude that determines how you will interprete and respond to situations"; examples of its synonyms are "mentality", "outlook" etc. (thefreedictionary.com)

2. Self-esteem

"A realistic respect for, or favourable impression of oneself; self-respect." (Dictionary.com).

Your mindset and you

Your mindset determines your thought-flow. Thoughts are very powerful as they are capable of shaping what happens, or does not happen to a person.

Also, your mindset affects your self-esteem and general lifestyle - your way of life, conduct, habits, or behaviour, and the level of respect you have for yourself. Your mindset defines you.

In view of the above, we can safely say that

the way you think determines:

- What you do and say; or will not do or say.

- Your motives for what you do or say; or will not do or say.

- Your level of self-confidence; that is, how confident you are, or otherwise.

- How you allow other people to treat you; what is acceptable or unacceptable to you about how people treat you.

- How you interpret what others do to you; or fail to do.

- How you respond to other people's action or inaction; the extent to which you are able to absorb it, or allow it to affect you.

- How you interpret life's challenges and difficulties.

- How you respond to life's trials; that is, how you react under pressure.

- How you treat other people, especially the people in your life – spouse, children, siblings etc. For example, a person with low self-esteem may treat the people in his or her life with little or no respect!

- Your sense of self-worth, or otherwise.

This means that how you think will determine whether you will have a balanced self-esteem (healthy self-worth); a low self-esteem (inferiority complex); or a high self-esteem (superiority complex).

Yes, your mindset will also determine:

- The choices you make in terms of friends, associations, career, life-partner etc.

- Your level of productivity at work, at home, and other life's endeavours.

- Your belief system; or sense of right and wrong.

- Your decisions on specific situations on life's path.

- Your outlook on life; that is, how you view life, and life's situations.

Your Mindset is you!

The Bible says, *"For as he thinks in his heart, so is he ...."* (Proverbs 23:7a). The state of your heart determines your mind-set; and this in turn determines your thought flow.

Also, your thought flow determines your actions (or inactions), and these determine your habit (what you do regularly); your habit becomes your character; and your character is you!

Renew your mind

In view of the above, we can safely say that your mindset determines many things about you. For a healthy mindset, the Bible's admonition is:

"... do not be conformed to this world, but <u>be transformed by the renewing of your mind</u>, that you may prove what is that good and acceptable and perfect will of God." Romans 12:2 (Emphasis mine).

The "tonic" for your mind's renewal is the Word of God. *"Your word I have hidden in my heart, that I might not sin against You, O Lord."* Psalm 119:11.

When you regularly study, meditate and obey God's Word, your heart is purified and renewed; and by extension, your mindset.

A renewed mindset helps you to conform to the image of Christ, rather than the deadly worldly pattern. Therefore, constantly renew your mind to renew your life.

Conclusion

A regular dose of God's Word keeps your heart in good shape, and this constantly keeps your mind renewed. Therefore, it is not surprising that the Bible says:

"Keep your heart with all diligence, for out of it spring the issues of life." Proverbs 4:23.

12
Your Mindset and Prayers

Introduction

As mentioned in the previous Chapter, your mind-set determines many things about you, and this includes your prayer life - how you will pray, what you will pray for, and what you will receive from God. This is the aim of this Chapter.

Five case-studies from the Bible

(a). Mrs Hannah Elkanah (1 Samuel 1:1-28; 2:1-11 & 18-21).

(b). General Naaman of Syria (2 Kings 5:1-19).

(c). The Syrophoenician Woman (Mark 7:24-30).

(d). Blind Bartimaeus the beggar (Mark 10:46-52).

(e). The crippled man at the Beautiful Gate (Acts 3:1-10).

Mrs Hannah Elkanah

(1 Samuel 1:1-28; 2:1-11 & 18-21).

"Now there was a certain man of Ramathaim Zophim... his name was Elkanah... and he had two wives; the name of one was Hannah, and the name of the other was Peninnah. Peninnah had children, but Hannah had no children... and her rival also provoked her severely, to make her miserable.... So it was, year by year, when she went up to the house of the Lord, that she provoked her; therefore, she wept and did not eat." 1 Samuel 1:1-7.

Mrs Hannah Elkanah was:

- Miserable

She felt miserable and hopeless as a result of the issue of childlessness in her life; coupled with incessant severe provocation from Peninah.

- Depressed

She was sad and depressed; at times she wept so much that she lost her appetite for food.

A changed Mindset

When Hannah was sad and depressed, her situation remained the same year in year out. However, when her mindset changed from that of sorrow and depression, she received strength to take positive action.

She had faith that God could help her, and so poured her heart to the Lord in prayer. This was the beginning of a new lease of life for her.

"So Hannah arose after they had finished eating and drinking in Shiloh.... And she was in bitterness of soul, and prayed to the Lord and wept in anguish.

Then she made a vow and said, O Lord of hosts, if you will indeed look on the affliction of your maidservant and remember me, and not forget Your maidservant, but will give Your maidservant a male child, then I will give him to the Lord all the days of his life....

So the woman went her way and ate, and her face was no longer sad .... And Elkanah knew Hannah his wife, and the Lord remembered her.... Hannah conceived and bore a son, and called his name Samuel, saying, "Because I asked for him from the Lord." 1 Samuel 1:9-20.

A further Analysis

Mrs Hannah Elkanah's changed mindset produced *good traits worthy of emulation,* and below are some of them:

- **A strong faith in God**

She trusted that God could put away her reproach and make her fruitful; hence she went to God in prayers.

- **Casting one's care upon God**

She no longer allowed her challenges to make her depressed; she cast it to the Lord in prayers according to 1 Peter 5:7 which says:*"Casting all your care upon Him, for He cares for you."*

- **Strong determination for change**

Mrs Hannah Elkanah was strongly determined to have a change of story. She fervently poured her heart to God in prayer; and Pastor Eli thought she was drunk.

She did not get offended at the wrong accusation, nor allowed it to weary her in the place of prayers (1 Samuel 1:12-18); offence might have hindered her prayers.

- **Being joyous during trials**

After Hannah cast her burden upon the Lord, she believed that God has granted her request. Even though she has not seen the physical manifestation, it was on record that:

"... the woman went her way and ate, and her face was no longer sad." 1 Samuel 1:18b.

- **Faithfulness to one's vow to God**

After the physical manifestation of Hannah's prayer request, which was the birth of Samuel; she fulfilled her vow to give Samuel to the Lord throughout his life.

"... I will take him, that he may appear before the Lord and remain there forever.... When she has weaned him, she took him up with her... and brought him to the house of the Lord in Shiloh... and brought the child to Eli.

And she said.... For this child I prayed, and the Lord has granted me my petition which I asked of Him. Therefore I also have lent him to the Lord; as long as He lives he shall be lent to the Lord. So they worshipped the Lord there." 1 Samuel 1:22-28.

For fulfilling her vows, God blessed Hannah with five other children; three sons and two daughters.

"... the child ministered to the Lord before Eli the priest.... And Eli would bless Elkanah and his wife, and say, "the Lord give you descendants from this woman for the loan that was given to the Lord.".... And the Lord visited Hannah, so that she conceived and bore three sons and two daughters. Meanwhile the child Samuel grew before the Lord." 1 Samuel 2:11; 20 &21.

This is very Important

- **Promptly fulfil your vows**

As Christians, we should be like Hannah, by <u>promptly</u> fulfilling any vow we make to God in the place of prayers; or for whatever reason.

"When you make a vow to God, do not delay to pay it; for He has no pleasure in fools, pay what you have vowed – better not to vow than to vow and not pay." Ecclesiastes 5:4 & 5.

- **Keep your marital vows!**

As Christians, it is also very important for us to fulfil our marital vows to our respective spouses (by being faithful to each other); this brings glory to God.

We should refuse to betray each other through adultery; or in whatever way. The Almighty God equates marital unfaithfulness with treachery! Very serious, isn't it?

"... You cover the altar of the Lord with tears, with weeping and crying; so He does not regard the offering anymore, nor receive it with goodwill from your hands. Yet you say , "For what reason?" Because the Lord had been witness between you and the wife of your youth, with whom you have dealt treacherously; yet she is your companion and your wife by covenant... Therefore take heed to your spirit, and let none deal treacherously with the wife of his youth." Malachi 2:13-15.

We can safely infer from the above verses that the Almighty God also expects the Christian wife to be faithful to the "husband of her youth".

- **Avoid Unkindness**

We should avoid being unkind like Peninnah, but rather be empathetic with those going through trials, do something to ease their pains; and thereby put smiles on their faces. The Bible says:

"Bear one another's burdens, and so fulfil the law of Christ." Galatians 6:2.

- **Praise God for His blessings**

Christians ought to constantly give God praise for His blessings on us, always remembering that we are what we are by the grace of God; and therefore refuse to oppress those who are less-privileged than us.

For Sober Reflections

The evil of polygyny is seen in the situation of rivalry and disharmony in the family of the Elkanahs.

While Samuel positively affected his generation for God, there was no mention of any achievement from Peninnah's children.

General Naaman of Syria

(2 Kings 5:1-19).

"Now Naaman, commander of the army of the king of Syria, was a great and honourable man in the eyes of his master, because by him the Lord had given victory to Syria. He was also a mighty man of valour, but a leper." 2 Kings 5:1.

General Naaman was a valiant and respectable Army Officer who had fought and won many battles for his master; but he was a leper. The Israelite househelp of Mrs Naaman told her of the Prophet in Israel who could heal her husband.

Mrs Naaman told General Naaman about it, and arrangements were concluded for the journey. He was given a letter by his king to the king of Israel; he also went with his aides, and gifts of:

"... ten talents of silver, six thousand shekels of gold, and ten changes of clothing." 2 Kings 5:5.

On reaching Prophet Elisha, the man of God sent his messenger to General Naaman to go and wash seven times in the Jordan river.

"Then Naaman went with his horses and chariot, and he stood at the door of Elisha's house. And Elisha sent a messenger to him, saying "Go and wash in the Jordan seven times, and your flesh shall be restored to you, and you shall be clean."

But Naaman became furious, and went away and said, "Indeed, I said to myself, he will surely come out to me, and stand and call on the name of the Lord his God, and wave his hand over the place, and heal the leprousy'.

Are not the Abanah and the Pharpar, the rivers of Damascus, better than all the waters of Israel? Could I not wash in them and be clean? So he turned and went away in a rage." 2 Kings 5:9-12.

General Naaman was:

- **Narrow-minded**

He had a pre-conceived idea of how the healing process should be; that the man of God should come out to him, lay hands on the leprous spot, and pray over it.

"... I said to myself, he will surely come out to me, and stand and call on the name of the Lord his God, and wave his hand over the place, and heal the leprousy'" 2 Kings 5:11.

General Naaman's narrow-mindedness resulted in him showing traces of:

- **Pride.**

Naaman was so full of himself, his position and achievements that he felt insulted that a messenger was sent to receive him. He expected the man of God to personally welcome him, and minister to him.

"And Elisha sent a messenger to him, saying "Go and wash in the Jordan seven times, and your flesh shall be restored to you, and you shall be clean. But Naaman became furious...." 2 Kings 5:10-11a.

- **Offence**

It was glaring that he was disappointed and offended that the Prophet Elisha did not come out to meet him.

- **Anger**

Having allowed offence to take root, Naaman became very angry that he turned away from the purpose of his journey to Israel; which was to receive healing!

"... Naaman became furious, and went away ... he turned and went away in a rage." 2 Kings 5:11-12.

- **Ethnocentric tendency**

The word "ethnocentric" has been used here to mean "characterized by or based on the attitude that one's group is superior". (Merriam-Webster Dictionary).

It is very likely that the Syrians had a mindset that they were superior to the Israelites. The tone of the letter written by the Syrian king to the king of Israel, coupled with the latter's response suggest this.

"Then the king of Syria said, "Go now, and I will send a letter to the king of Israel... then he brought the letter to the king of Israel, which said, Now be advised, when this

letter comes to you, that I have sent Naaman my servant to you, that you may heal him of his leprosy... when the king of Israel read the letter,... he tore his clothes...." 2 Kings 5:5-7.

General Naaman showed this ethnocentric tendency when he said: *"Are not the Abanah and the Pharpar, the rivers of Damascus, better than all the waters of Israel? Could I not wash in them and be clean? So he turned and went away in a rage."* 2 Kings 5:12.

Further Explanations

The request letter sent to the king of Israel for General Naaman's healing is comparable to making a prayer request to God, the King of kings!

However, the above-mentioned negative mindset would have robbed Naaman of the answer to this "prayer request" if not for the wise counsel of his aides.

"And his servants came near and spoke to him, and said, "My father, if the prophet had told you to do something great, would you not have done it? How much more then, when he says to you, 'wash, and be clean'?

So he went down and dipped seven times in the Jordan, according to the saying of the man of God; and his flesh was restored like the flesh of a little child, and he was clean." 2 Kings 5:13 & 14.

A changed Mindset

The counsel from Naaman's servants gave Naaman a new orientation that relieved him of his negative attitudes. This gave him a healthy mindset which produced *good traits worthy of emulation*. Some of these are:

- **Humility**

It was humble of him to have reasoned with his subordinates Officers, and thereby embraced their better counsel.

- **Obedience**

He did according to the Prophet's instruction to go and wash seven times in the River Jordan. Obedience brought the required answer to his "prayer request"; General Naman was healed of his leprosy!

- **Gratitude**

With a heart of gratitude, Naaman went back to Prophet Elisha to inform the latter of his healing.

- **Worship**

He did not "worship" man, but acknowledged the Almighty God as the Healer; and gave God all the glory.

"And he returned to the man of God, he and his aides, ... and he said, "Indeed, now I know that there is no God in all the earth, except in Israel...." 2 Kings 5:15.

- **He chose the living God**

Naaman chose to serve only the living God of Israel; he told Prophet Elisha *"... your servant will no longer offer either burnt offering or sacrifice to other gods, but to the Lord."* 2 Kings 5:17.

This means that General Naaman received the miracle, and the Miracle Worker!

13
Your Mindset and Prayers
(Continued)

The Syro-Phoenician Woman

(Mark 7:24-30).

The story of the Syro-Phoenician woman is a typical example of intercessory prayers. She heard that Jesus Christ was in her neighbourhood, and came to plead for the healing of her demon-possessed daughter.

"... He arose and went to the region of Tyre and Sidon. And He entered a house and wanted no one to know it,

but He could not be hidden. For a woman whose young daughter had an unclean spirit heard about Him, and she came and fell at His feet. The woman was a Greek, a Syro-Phoenician by birth, and she kept asking Him to cast the demon out of her daughter." Mark 7:24-26.

Here is the response of our Lord Jesus Christ to her: *"But Jesus said to her, "Let the children be filled first, for it is not good to take the children's bread and throw it to the little dogs."* Mark 7:27.

However, this anonymous woman was not put off:

And she answered and said to Him, Yes, Lord, yet even the little dogs under the table eat from the children's crumbs."

Then He said to her, "For this saying go your way; the demon has gone out of your daughter." And when she had come to her house, she found the demon gone out, and her daughter lying on the bed." Mark 7:28-30.

The Syro-Phoenician woman's good traits worthy of emulation:

- **A heart of Worship**

As soon as the Syro-Phoenician woman came to Jesus Christ, she fell in worship before Him. Afterwards, she presented her "prayer request" of intercession for her daughter.

"... a woman whose young daughter had an unclean spirit heard about Him, and she came and fell at His feet. The woman was a Greek, a Syro-Phoenician by

birth, and she kept asking Him to cast the demon out of her daughter." Mark 7:25 & 26.

- **Humility**

She humbled herself before our Lord Jesus Christ by falling at His feet in <u>true</u> worship!

- **Great faith**

She had great faith in Jesus Christ, that He has power to heal her demon-possessed daughter; hence she "interceded" on her behalf.

- **No offence**

Even when Jesus Christ said that the children's food ought not be given to little dogs, she was not offended. Remember that offences are blockages to prayers.

- **Persistent 'praying'**

In spite of Jesus Christ's reply to her, this woman persisted in her request for her daughter's healing; she refused to be discouraged.

"And she answered and said to Him, Yes, Lord, yet even the little dogs under the table eat from the children's crumbs" Mark 7:28.

A Further Analysis

As a result of the woman's importunity, humility, and great faith; her request was granted; our Lord Jesus Christ pronounced the girl healed.

"... For this saying go your way; the demon has gone out of your daughter." And when she had come to her house, she found the demon gone out...." Mark 7:29 & 30.

Blind Bartimaeus

(Mark 10:46-52).

"... blind Bartimaeus ... sat by the road begging. And when he heard that it was Jesus of Nazareth, he began to cry out and say, "Jesus, Son of David, have mercy on me!"

Then many warned him to be quiet; but he cried out all the more, "Son of David, have mercy on me!" So Jesus stood still and commanded him to be called. Then they called the blind man, saying to him, "Be of good cheer. Rise, He is calling you". And throwing aside his garment, he rose and came to Jesus.

So Jesus answered and said to him, "What do you want Me to do for you?" The blind man said to him, "Rabboni, that I may receive my sight."

Then Jesus said to him, "Go your way; your faith has made you well." And immediately he received his sight and followed Jesus on the road." Mark 10:46-52.

Blind Bartimaeus' good traits worthy of emulation:

- **A healthy mindset**

He didn't allow his negative circumstances to narrow his mindset to a life of perpetual begging; he strongly preferred to be healed rather than alms-begging (vv.46 & 47).

- **Implicit faith in God**

He believed that Jesus Christ had the power to heal; he therefore "prayed" that Jesus Christ will show him mercy.

"... when he heard that it was Jesus of Nazareth, he began to cry out and say, "Jesus, Son of David, have mercy on me!" Mark 10:47.

- **Strong determination**

Bartimaeus didn't merely desire a change from his blind and beggarly situation; he strongly pursued it.

He was strongly determined to receive his sight, become free and independent. This made him to be undeterred by the hostile attitude of the crowd to silence him.

"Then many warned him to be quiet; but he cried out all the more, "Son of David, have mercy on me!" (Acts 10:48) .

- **Persistent 'praying'**

He persistently asked Jesus Christ to heal him despite the negative attitude of the crowd to silence him (verse 48). This yielded a positive result as Jesus Christ gave him the needed attention.

- **Being specific about his request**

When Jesus Christ asked him what he wanted, he said *"... that I may receive my sight."* (Mark 10:51b). This was granted by our Lord Jesus Christ.

"Then Jesus said to him, "Go your way; your faith has made you well...." Mark 10:52a.

- **Becoming a follower of Christ**

After receiving his miracle, he didn't turn away from Jesus Christ, but followed Him; he wanted both the miracle and the Miracle Worker.

"... And immediately he received his sight and followed Jesus on the road." Mark 10: 52b.

The Crippled Man at the Beautiful Gate

(Acts 3:1-10).

"... a certain man lame from his mother's womb was carried, whom they laid daily at the gate of the temple which is called beautiful, to ask alms from those who entered the temple; who seeing Peter and John about to go into the temple, asked for alms.

And fixing His eyes on him, with John, Peter said, "Look at us." So he gave them his attention, expecting to receive something from them." Acts 3:2 – 5.

The crippled man was:

- **Beggarly-minded**

Having been used to begging from those coming into the Temple, his expectation did not go beyond that when he saw Peter and John. *"... seeing Peter and John about to go into the temple, asked for alms."* Acts 3:3.

- **Narrowly-minded**

This unnamed adult beggar was born lame and so must have been at the Beautiful Gate for a long time.

The negative circumstances around him narrowed his mindset to the daily routine of begging, that he couldn't think of a "better life" beyond the Beautiful Gate!

It wasn't the crippled beggar alone who was narrow-minded, but also, his people. The best they did for him was to daily "help" him get to the Temple gate for alms-begging.

"... a certain man lame from his mother's womb was carried, whom they laid daily at the gate of the temple which is called beautiful, to ask alms from those who entered the temple." Acts 3:2.

Our merciful God

However, despite the narrow mindset of the crippled man, God showed him mercy by healing him through Peter and John. This is not to encourage narrow-mindedness, but rather to show how compassionate God is.

"Then Peter said, Silver and gold I do not have, but what I do have I give you: in the name of Jesus Christ of Nazareth, rise up and walk. And he took him by the right hand and lifted him up, and immediately his feet and ankle bones received strength." Acts 3:6 & 7.

God did for him more than the "silver or gold" he was expecting from Peter and John. God healed him, and thereby put an end to limitations in his life.

Please Note: If not for God's mercy, this formerly crippled man would have remained a beggar for life. This wouldn't have been because God could not heal him; but because of his narrow mindset.

A Further Analysis

However, this formerly blind beggar had *good traits worthy of emulation;* and some of these are:

- **He was not irritable**

When the crippled beggar saw Peter and John, he begged them for alms, and was expecting to receive money from them. However:

"... Peter said, "Look at us." So he gave them his attention, expecting to receive something from them. "Then Peter said, Silver and gold I do not have ...." Acts 3:4 – 6a.

Peter's declaration that there was no money did not make the beggar angry; otherwise, he might have missed out on his healing.

- **He had faith in God**

The crippled beggar was not put off when money was not forthcoming from Peter and John. This must have prepared him to "hear" Peter's next statement; that He should get up in the Name of Jesus Christ.

He had faith that it could be done, and he was healed; thereby receiving much more than he ever thought or expected.

"... what I do have I give you: in the name of Jesus Christ of Nazareth, rise up and walk. And he took him by the right hand and lifted him up, and immediately his feet and ankle bones received strength." Acts 3:6 & 7.

- **He had great joy**

On receiving his healing, the former lame beggar was full of joy. This could be expected from a man who was lame from his mother's womb. For the first time (I presume), he had a taste of real joy!

- **He offered praise to God**

He was thankful to God for the divine encounter that brought his healing. He did not give the praise to

Peter and John; but gave the praise to the One Who owns it all - the Almighty God.

"So he, leaping up, stood and walked and entered the temple with them – walking, leaping and praising God." Acts 3:8.

- **He remained with God**

He didn't abandon the Miracle Worker after receiving His miracle. He *"... entered the temple with them – walking, leaping and praising God."* Acts 3:8b.

The healing of the crippled man must have inspired others to put their trust in the living God; both at that time, and down the ages. This unnamed man became a source of wonder and amazement (Acts 3:9 & 10b).

Your Mindset and prayers

Your mindset is very important as you come to God in prayers. It will determine the extent to which you will trust God, how you will pray, what you will pray for; what you will expect, and will eventually receive from God.

A Christian with a narrow mindset is limited in the place of prayers. This is not because God could not do great things, but one's narrow mindset puts a ceiling on what you ask in prayers; and what you receive from God.

An example that readily comes to mind is that, the negative mindset of unbelief limited what the people of Nazareth could benefit from Jesus Christ's Ministry.

"... Jesus said to them, "A prophet is not without honour except in his own country and in his own house." Now He did not do many mighty works there because of their unbelief." Matthew 13:57 & 58.

How is your mindset?

In view of the above, I ask you this important question "How is your mindset?" Is it healthy like that of blind Bartimaeus, and the Syro-Phoenician woman?

Perhaps it is narrow like that of the crippled man; determined by your negative life's circumstances and experiences? This puts a limit on you in the place of prayers. However, you can have a changed mindset like Mrs Hannah Elkanah, and General Naaman.

When one's mindset is determined by God's faithfulness and His infallible Word, (rather than one's challenges); you open your life to the limitless possibilities available in God, and through God!

The Bible says: *"And whatever things you ask in prayer, believing, you will receive."* Matthew 21:22.

Conclusion

Your mindset is you! *"For as he thinks in his heart, so is he ...."* (Proverbs 23:7a). A healthy mindset means a "healthy you"; and an unhealthy mindset means an "unhealthy you". Therefore, guard your heart diligently to safeguard your mindset.

To sustain a healthy mindset, one's mind must be continually renewed by God's Word. A healthy mindset produces a healthy Christian; and the more Christ-like the Christian is, the more effective your prayers become.

14
Seek the Mind of God

The Christian needs to regularly know the mind of God for every aspect of one's life; including what to pray for.

As mentioned in an earlier Chapter, Christians need to be keenly sensitive to the Holy Spirit while praying. This will help us to avoid praying for what is not God's best for us. The Bible says:

"Trust in the Lord with all your heart, and lean not on your own understanding; in all your ways acknowledge Him, and He shall direct your paths." Proverbs 3:5 & 6.

Knowing God's Mind

This is used here to mean praying in accordance with the will of God. This will enable us to pray aright, and enjoy God's best for us.

Therefore, as you go to God in prayers, it is very important to seek the mind of God; to ask for His perfect will concerning your needs and requests. This helps us to pray in alignment with His will.

The need for God's Mind

Christians need to seek God's Mind because as mere mortals, we are limited in our understanding. On the other hand, our God is limitless in understanding; and unfathomable in His wisdom. His thoughts and ways are higher than ours!

"For My thoughts are not your thoughts, nor are your ways My ways," says the Lord. For as the heavens are higher than the earth, so are My ways higher than your ways, and My thoughts than your thoughts." Isaiah 55:8 & 9.

God sees the whole picture of things; and knows the end from the beginning. *"As for God, His way is perfect...."* (Psalm 18:30a). He is the only One Who can guide us (through His Holy Spirit) to pray aright.

Therefore, it is very important for Christians to seek the mind of God; so as to know the appropriate prayer requests to present to Him.

Benefits of knowing God's Mind

When one seeks God's face to know His will as per what to ask in prayers, It...

- Helps us to pray aright, and have God's best for us, our loved ones, the Church; the society, and our generation.

- Saves us from wasting time on praying outside the will of God.

- Shields us from the disappointment of "unanswered prayers". The Bible says: *"You ask and do not receive, because you ask amiss...."* James 4:3a.

- Protects us from the attendant avoidable heartaches of having less than God's best for us; or what will send leanness to our souls! *"And He gave them their request, but sent leanness into their soul."* Psalm 106:15.

Conclusion

As we go to God in prayers, we should always seek His guidance concerning His perfect will for our lives; so that we can pray aright. A consistent spiritual growth will enable us to know what to pray for as the need arises.

15
No 'Plan B'

Introduction

In the preceding Chapter, we have seen the need to seek God's Mind before presenting our prayer requests to Him. Therefore, once you are sure that what you are praying for agrees with God's will, let there be no 'Plan B'!

However, our motive for asking should be right, which is to glorify God; and not for self-aggrandisement, or any other selfish reasons.

Conceptual Clarification

The phrase "no plan "B" is used here to mean:

(1). If you are sure that your prayer requests align with God's perfect will, plan and purpose for your life; keep presenting your requests to God.

Even when situations seem "hopeless", and the physical manifestation of your requests seems to linger, refuse to shift ground as per your prayers.

(2). That there should be no "alternative" as to one's Source of help. *"Our help is in the Name of the Lord, Who made heaven and earth."* Psalm124:8.

Our God is great, mighty and trustworthy. Like the Psalmist, let your resolve be: *"My soul, wait silently for God alone, for my expectation is from Him."* Psalm 62:5.

No 'Plan B'!

Having a plan "B" will distract you from your prayer requests; and may also weaken your hand in the place of prayers.

Also, trying to seek "help" outside of God will only lead to frustrations and disappointments; whether in the short or long run. The Bible says: *"Their sorrows shall be multiplied who hasten after another god...."* Psalm 16:4.

A Necessary Explanation

As you pray, there are times you need to take physical steps to have the physical manifestation of your requests; e.g. a student praying to excel must couple hard work with prayers; otherwise, success becomes elusive.

In as much as prayer is still relevant to academic success (for only God can give wisdom and understanding); hard work is a must because *"... faith by itself, if it does not have works, is dead."* James 2:17.

Another example is when a person praying for healing requires medical care, such should go for it. When one receives medical care, it is only God that can make it effective; so, in a way, it is still God Who heals.

The Doctors are doing a great job. They often try their best, and leave the rest to God Who has the final say in all things; hence their common slogan "We care, God heals."

However, where the Doctor's report says there is no hope for you; you can hold on to God in prayers, to bring healing out of your seemingly hopeless situation.

The Almighty God is still in the business of healing people divinely; and will continue to heal people divinely. *"For with God nothing will be impossible."* Luke 1:37.

Conclusion

God owns all the power in Heaven and on Earth, and He is in control of all things in His Universe. Prayers are answered at His discretion, and in His Own timing.

Therefore, Christians should always trust God for interventions in their situations; and patiently wait for Him. He is our only Source of help!

"... From whence comes my help? My help comes from the Lord, Who made heaven and earth." Psalm 121: 1 & 2.

As we constantly look up to God for help, we can never be put to shame. God says: *"... no one who waits for My help will be disappointed."* Isaiah 49:23c (GNB).

16
Pray God's Word

The Word of God is alive and active; and so, it is a boost to prayers. Therefore, we are to pray using God's Word. *"For the Word of God is living and active and full of power [making it operative, energising, and effective] ...."* Hebrews 4:12a (AMP).

Please Note: I am not talking of using the Psalms to pray, but using God's Word generally; whether Psalms, or any of the other Books of the Bible.

Search the Scriptures

As you go to God in prayers, find the appropriate Word of God that addresses your need, and use it to pray. That is, use God's Word to present your prayer requests to God.   For example, the following Scriptures can be used when praying for:

- **The salvation of our beloved ones; or people you have preached to.**

"... As surely as I, the Sovereign Lord, am the living God, I do not enjoy seeing sinners die. I would rather see them stop sinning and live...." Ezekiel 33:11 (GNB).

Also, it is written, *"Do you think I enjoy seeing an evil person die?" asks the Sovereign Lord. "No, I would rather see him repent and live."* Ezekiel 18:23 (GNB).

The above verses show that God does not enjoy seeing sinners die in their sins. Therefore, if we fervently pray to God for the salvation of the unsaved, He will touch their hearts, and save their souls.

- **The backslider; or personal victory over besetting sins.**

"Can the spoils of war be taken from the mighty man, or the captives of a tyrant be rescued? Indeed, this is what the Lord says, "even the captives of the mighty man will be taken away, and the tyrant's spoils of war will be rescued...." Isaiah 49:24-25a (AMP).

- **Waiters on the Lord for the fruit of the womb.**

"No one shall suffer miscarriage or be barren in your land...." Exodus 23:26.

"... there shall not be a male or female barren among you or among your livestock." Deuteronomy 7:14.

Even, our livestock is not left out in the promise!

Also, *"There is no one like the Lord our God... He honours the childless wife in her home; He makes her happy by giving her children."* Psalm 113:5 & 9 (GNB).

- **Healing**

"... He was wounded for our transgressions, He was bruised for our iniquities; the chastisement for our peace was upon Him, and <u>by His stripes we are healed."</u> Isaiah 53:5 (Emphasis mine).

Also, the Almighty God says, *"... I am the Lord who heals you."* Exodus 15:26.

- **Provision**

Perhaps your financial situation is in a mess, and there are outstanding bills to be paid? Maybe you are in debt; or you need provision for an urgent need in your life, Home or Ministry? etc. The Almighty God is our Source, and His Word says:

"And my God shall supply all your need according to His riches in glory by Christ Jesus." Philippians 4:19.

It is very important to note that God will supply our "need" (or necessities); and not neccesarily our "want" (or indulgencies).

- **Wisdom**

"If any of you lacks wisdom, let him ask God, who gives to all liberally and without reproach, and it will be given to him." James 1:5.

As Christians, we need wisdom for every aspect of life; in our academics, careers, businesses, home building, child-rearing, social interactions, trials and challenges etc.

This is very Important!

The promises of God have conditions attached to them; and that is, obedience to His Word. The Bible says:

"... If you diligently obey the voice of the Lord your God, to observe carefully all His commandments... the Lord your God will set you high above all nations of the earth... blessed shall you be...." Deuteronomy 28:1 & 2.

You may wish to read the whole Chapter of Deuteronomy 28 to see the blessings of obedience; and the curses that accompany disobedience to God's Word.

Conclusion

When we pray using God's Word, this gives a boost to our prayers. As one maintains a steady growth in Christ, God will show us the appropriate Scriptures for our needs as we run the race Home.

17
Be Unreasonable

Introduction

The phrase "be unreasonable" has been used here to mean, when you come to God in prayers, don't try to reason out how God will do it; rather, just take God at His Word. The Almighty God says:

"For as the rain comes down, and the snow from heaven, and do not return there, but water the earth, and make it bring forth and bud, that it may give seed to the sower and bread to the eater, so shall My Word be that goes forth from My mouth; it shall not return to Me void, but it shall accomplish what I please, and it shall prosper in the thing for which I sent it." Isaiah 55:10 & 11.

Therefore, when you come to God in prayers, always have at the back of your mind that:

- **God is Almighty**

This is God's testimony of Himself: *"… The Lord appeared to Abram and said to him, I am the Almighty God…."* Genesis 17:1.

- **Nothing is too hard for God**

The Almighty God owns all the power in Heaven and on Earth, and so nothing is too hard for Him. God says: *"Behold, I am the Lord, the God of all flesh. Is there anything too hard for Me?"* Jeremiah 32:27.

Also, it is written: *"Almighty Lord, You made heaven and earth by Your great strength and powerful arm. Nothing is too hard for You."* Jeremiah 32:17 (GW).

- **God's promises are Reliable**

The fact that nothing is too hard for God means He has the power to fulfil all He says; therefore, His promises are trustworthy.

"God is not a man, that He should lie, nor a son of man, that He should repent. Has He said, and will He not do? Or has He spoken, and will He not make it good?" Numbers 23:19.

- **God does as He pleases**

Yes, God does as He pleases, and no one can question Him. When God decides to do a thing, none can stop Him.

"... For I am God, and there is no other; I am God, and there is none like Me... My counsel shall stand, and I will do all My pleasure...." Isaiah 46:9 & 10.

Our God is trustworthy

In the light of all the above, we can safely put our trust in God and His Word; whether His Word from the Bible, or assurances received directly through the indwelling Holy Spirit.

"Blessed is she [he] who believed, for there will be a fulfilment of those things which were told her [him] from the Lord." Luke 1:45 [Emphasis added].

Dare to be Unreasonable!

The above-mentioned attributes of the Almighty God shows that Christians are in very safe Hand, so we can dare to be unreasonable in the place of prayers. Therefore:

1. Before you pray:

Don't try to reason out how God will answer your prayers, otherwise you may try to edit what you will pray for; or be discouraged from praying at all. Ours is to pray and trust God with the rest.

The Almighty God has given us a "blank cheque" to fill in our requests! How God will do it is none of our business. Once you are sure your requests align with God's will for you, go ahead to ask God.

"Ask, and it will be given to you; seek, and you will find; knock, and it will be opened to you. For everyone who asks receives, and he who seeks finds, and to him who knocks it will be opened." Matthew 7:7 & 8.

2. After you have prayed:

Don't try to figure out how God will do it; so that your faith will not be "punctured"; otherwise defeat is certain!

Therefore, to safeguard your faith, and the physical manifestation of your requests, just believe God's Word that: *"... Whatever things you ask when you pray, believe that you receive them, and you will have them."* Mark 11:24.

3. Also, after you have prayed:

Don't attempt to reason out how the answers will come; if not, when it comes, you may not recognise it. An example was when the disciples were praying for Peter's release from prison in Acts 12:1-19.

When the physical manifestation of their prayers came, they couldn't believe it (See Acts 12:11-17). Perhaps, they were thinking if Peter would be released, it was likely to be during the daytime; and not in the dead of the night!

As earlier mentioned, the Almighty God does as He pleases, and no one can question Him.

Also, God is predictable in His faithfulness, but unpredictable in His ways; in how He does whatever He purposes to do. He has myriad of ways He can choose to answer our prayers and petitions; so, let us quit reasoning it out.

"Oh, the depth of the riches both of the wisdom and knowledge of God! How unsearchable are His judgments and His ways past finding out!" Romans 11:33.

4. After receiving God's Word of assurance:

When you have received assurance from God that your prayers have been answered, but you are yet to see the physical manifestation, hold tightly to God's promises.

No matter how the physical situation looks; don't allow the assurance you have received to slip away from you. Let it be settled in your heart that it is done. *"For with God nothing will be impossible."* Luke 1:37.

Begin to think and plan like somebody who already have whatever you prayed for; for example, if you have prayed for healing, and God has assured you it is done; believe that you have excellent health, no matter the situation in the physical.

Another example is, when you have prayed to God for the fruit of the womb. If you have received God's assurance that it is done, begin to buy baby's items!

Yes, buy baby items with a strong conviction that the babies that will use them will soon arrive. No matter how long it seems before their arrival, don't shift ground as per your God-given conviction.

You should see the victory and glory in the midst of the trials because: *"God is not a man, that He should lie, nor a son of man, that He should repent. Has He said, and will He not do? Or has He spoken, and will He not make it good?"* Numbers 23:19.

5. After receiving the physical manifestation:

When you have received the physical manifestation of your prayers, don't allow it to be "stolen" from you for whatever reason.

Be watchful, and continually secure your blessings by covering them with prayers, and the precious Blood of Jesus Christ, which is our "spiritual insurance cover".

Also, secure yourself (Spirit, Soul and Body); your loved ones, converts, mentees, belongings etc. with this precious Blood of Jesus Christ. The Blood line is the spiritual threshold that the devil dares not pass through.

"And they overcame him by the blood of the Lamb and by the word of their testimony...." Revelation 12:11a.

Limitless help from God

When we have "unreasonable faith" in God as we come before Him in prayers, there is no limit to what God can accomplish for us, and through us. Our God is Almighty; and He is:

"... able to do exceedingly abundantly above all we ask or think, according to the power that works in us, to Him

be glory in the Church by Christ Jesus to all generations, forever and ever. Amen." Ephesians 3:20 & 21.

Conclusion

The Almighty God is trustworthy, and His promises cannot fail. Therefore, whatever you ask God in prayers in absolute faith in Him, and in alignment with His will; you will surely receive.

"As for God, His way is perfect; the Word of the Lord is proven; He is a shield to all who trust in Him." Psalm 18:30.

18
No Negotiations

Introduction

One of the definitions of "negotiation" is: "discussion aimed at reaching an agreement." Some synonyms of Negotiations are: "talks, consultation(s), parleying, dialogue, bargaining etc. (dictionary.com).

The word "Negotiations" has been used here to mean "spiritual dialogues" aimed at reaching an agreement between the Christian and the devil, as per our prayer requests from God.

After you have prayed to God about your needs, the devil may whisper to you that your prayer request is a "tall order", and thereby try to convince you to edit it.

This negative suggestion can come when the situation of things seem hopeless; or the physical manifestation is not forthcoming as you expected.

No Negotiations!

Please, refuse to be open to any negotiations from the devil; remember that his three-fold ministry against you (and all Christians) is "... to *steal, and to kill, and to destroy...*" John 10:10a.

Glory be to God for the Gift of Jesus Christ who says: "*... I have come that they may have life, and that they may have it more abundantly.*" John 10: 10b.

Therefore, if you are sure you are praying in line with God's will, refuse to subject your requests to any negotiations; that is, have no talks, consultations, parleying, dialogues or bargaining with the devil.

As per your prayer requests, refuse to edit it; and don't stop praying. The Almighty God has assured us: "*Ask, and it will be given to you; seek, and you will find; knock, and it will be opened to you.*" Matthew 7:7.

No Surrender; No Retreat

As you continue to war in prayers:

- Refuse to entertain the editing of your prayer points; keep pressing in on your "tall order requests" until your joy is full.

- Don't give up on praying; and don't give up on God.

- Don't allow the tempo of your prayers to go down; instead, increase it.

Conclusion

Keep praying until your joy is full. As you persist in prayers with a stubborn faith in God, He will arise to your help in the nick of time.

19
Your 'help' is not Needed

Introduction

As Christians go to God in prayers, it is because we know we cannot help ourselves, and that only God can help us. The Bible says:

Yours, O Lord, is the greatness,

The power and the glory,

The victory and the majesty;

For all that is in heaven and in earth is Yours;

Yours is the Kingdom, O Lord,

And You are exalted as head over all.

Both riches and honour come from You,

And You reign over all.

In Your hand is power and might;

In Your hand it is to make great

And to give strength to all." 1 Chronicles 29:11-12.

God is Almighty

The Almighty God has power to help when we call on Him in prayers, and so doesn't need man's "help" to do whatever He purposes to do. Therefore, ours is just to pray, and then trust God with the rest.

"For I will not trust in my bow, nor shall my sword save me.... In God we boast all day long, and praise Your name forever." Psalm 44:6 & 8.

God's Intervention through Prayers

The Almighty God is the unequalled Expert in setting the stage to help His children. There are several examples in the Bible of how God intervened in the challenges of His children in answer to prayers. Some of these are:

The deliverance of the Israelites
(Esther Chapters 3-8)

Some Israelites were taken captive to Babylon; including Mordecai, and Esther his niece. Haman (one of the King's official) felt disrespected that Mordecai was not bowing in worship to him.

Therefore, he paid money into the King's Treasury for the destruction of all the Isrealites in Babylon.On receiving the bad news, Queen Esther and all Israelites fasted, and cried unto God to deliver them (Esther 4:3; 4:15 & 16).

In answer to prayers, the Almighty God turned the table against Haman, and delivered the Israelites from destruction; and the Israelites greatly rejoiced.

"The Jews had light and gladness, joy and honour ... the Jews had joy and gladness, a feast and a holiday. Then many of the people of the land became Jews, because fear of the Jews fell upon them." Esther 8:16 & 17.

The Rebuilding of Jerusalem
(The Book of Nehemiah)

Nehemiah was serving under King Artaxerxes of Babylon when news came to him, that Jerusalem, his fatherland was in ruins. Nehemiah was concerned; and_he prayed to God for His intervention and mercy.

"O Lord, I pray, please let Your ear be attentive to the prayer of Your servant... let Your servant prosper this day, I pray, and grant him mercy...." Nehemiah 1:11.

Afterwards he met King Artaxerxes for help. Nehemiah received favour (Nehemiah 2:1-6); "Visa" (Nehemiah 2:7); Provision (Nehemiah 2:8); and Security Guards from the King Artaxerxes (Nehemiah 2:9).

The Almighty God gave great grace to Nehemiah and his team; to build the broken walls of Jerusalem, despite stiff oppositions from Tobiah and Sanballat.

The rescue of Peter from prison (Acts 12:1-19)

Christians were being persecuted severely during the reign of King Herod. James was killed, and Peter was put in prison; with the intention of killing him after Passover.

And when Herod was about to bring him out, that night, Peter was sleeping, bound with two chains between two soldiers; and the guards before the door were keeping the prison.

However, the Church fervently cried unto God to rescue Peter from prison, and from death. "... *constant prayer was offered to God for him by the Church.*" Acts 12:5.

In answer to prayers, the Almighty God sent His Angel to miraculously rescue Peter from prison, and deliver him from death; to the joy of the brethren, and the glory of God.

The deliverance of Paul and Silas from prison (Acts 16:22-40)

Paul and Silas were imprisoned for the sake of the Gospel. They were not downcast; rather, they prayed and sang praises to God.

"But at midnight Paul and Silas were praying and singing hymns to God, and the prisoners were listening." Acts 16:25.

The Almighty God demonstrated His power so much that there was a great earthquake, the prison's foundations were shaken, all doors were opened; and everyone's chains were loosed! (See Acts 16:26).

The jailer was afraid, and wanted to kill himself, thinking the prisoners has escaped. However, Paul restrained him; and also assured him the prisoners were all there. (Acts 16:27 & 28).

The jailer fell down at the feet of Paul and Silas, ready to be saved; he and his household were ministered to; and they all believed in God.

The jailer cleaned the wounds of Paul and Silas, served them food; and they were later released from prison.

God will help you

The power of the Almighty God to help His children in their challenges is not limited to the Bible. God still answers prayers today, and will continue to answer prayers of faith presented to Him in the Name of Jesus Christ.

When you come to God in prayers with simple child-like trust, He will arise to help you. The Bible says: *"And whatever things you ask in prayer, believing, you will receive."* Matthew 21:22.

The Almighty God will fulfil His promise, and so will surely help you; none can stop Him from doing whatever He wants to do.

Don't get in the way!

In view of the above, the Almighty God doesn't need our "help" to do whatever He wants to do for us in answer to our prayers. Therefore, don't try to control or "manipulate" things; otherwise, one will mess things up!

As earlier mentioned, ours is to pray, and trustingly leave the rest to the Almighty God; to do what He alone can do. You can be assured that God will *"... do exceedingly abundantly above all we ask or think...."* Ephesians 3:20.

Conclusion

As the Christian goes to God in prayers, one should always remember that He has the power to answer our prayers which are in alignment with His will for us. God is the Almighty; and with Him *"... nothing shall be impossible."* Luke 1:37.

20
Reject all Contrary Voices

The phrase "contrary voices" is used here to mean every suggestion that is intended to attack your prayer requests, and weaken your faith in God; so as to "abort " your expected testimonies! This can come in the form of:

- **Doubt**

When you are filled with doubts, your prayers will be obstructed!

"… for he who doubts is like a wave of the sea driven and tossed by the wind. For let not that man suppose that he will receive anything from the Lord…." James 1:6 & 7.

Therefore, whenever you are plagued by doubts, combat your doubts by delving into God's Word. This builds up your faith level.

- **Discouragement**

This can make you feel hopeless, and thereby shift your attention away from God. However, God is the only Source of help in the true sense of the word; and with no strings attached.

"The blessing of the Lord makes one rich, and adds no sorrow with it." Proverbs 10:22.

Whenever discouragement comes knocking, please, encourage yourself in the Lord like David. *"Now David was greatly distressed… but David strengthened himself in the Lord his God."* 1 Samuel 30:6.

- **Fear**

The spirit of fear may attack your mind; especially when the answer to prayers seem prolonged.

There could be the fear of the "unknown"; or fears that the answers may never come. Fear is not of God because," *… God has not given us the spirit of fear, but* *of power and of love and of a sound mind."* 2 Timothy 1:7.

In view of the above, refuse to give in to fear; more so *"... fear hath torment"* 1 John 4:18 (KJV).

- **Mockeries**

As a Christian, when you are going through trials, the devil can mock you through people; or directly through your thoughts.

You can be ridiculed with words like "if your God is powerful and caring, why didn't He answer your prayers?" etc. This is to discourage and weary you in the place of prayers.

Please, keep praying, keep trusting; and keep praying! The Almighty God will surely arise to defend His Name in your life in Jesus Name, Amen.

Like the Psalmist, let your declaration be: *"But as for me, I trust in You, O Lord; I say, "You are my God." My times are in Your hand..."* Psalm 31:14 & 15.

- **Accusation and Guilt**

As the Christian prays, voices of accusations may come; also, guilt feelings over one's past sins. These are meant to make you feel unworthy to stand before God, and to feel unqualified to receive from God. This is a subtle attack on your prayer life.

Whenever the devil torments you with your past sins; you should confidently arm yourself with the fact that Jesus Christ has paid the full price for your sins, has forgiven you; and has <u>disarmed</u>, <u>disgraced</u> and <u>defeated</u> him for you at Calvary (Colossians 2:13-15).

Also, the devil's future doom is a pointer to his eternal defeat. The Bible clearly says that there is *"... the everlasting fire prepared for the devil and his angels."* Matthew 25:41.

When you are armed with the above facts, you are emboldened to silence the devil. This loosens his grip over you; and helps you to confidently go back to your prayer closet.

Conclusion

You may not have control over the springing up of contrary voices; however, you can stop them from taking root in your heart. Rejecting all contrary voices, will enable you to persist in prayers against all odds.

21
Be at Rest in God

The Almighty God is the King of the whole Universe, and He alone has the power to help us . *"For God is the King of all the earth... God reigns over the nations; God sits on His holy throne."* Psalm 47: 7 & 8.

Therefore, when you have committed all your challenges to God in prayers, leave them there; and be at rest in God.

The President and the File

When a file is passed to the table of the President of a country, or the Chief Executive Officer (CEO) of a company; one will leave it there until a decision is taken on it. It is afterwards that action can be taken on the requests in the file.

By praying, you have passed the "file" of your prayer requests to God's "Table" for His attention; and the Almighty God is the real President! Therefore, leave the file there until God works on it, and turns your requests to testimonies.

Our Able Helper

During trials, always remember that you have the indwelling Holy Spirit to empower you to cope. Therefore, constantly tap from His inexhaustible grace!

Spiritual Building Blocks (SBB)

No trial is enjoyable when one is passing through it. However, our challenges will produce spiritual maturity in us; if we don't faint, and give up on God. Therefore, keep holding on, and be reminded that:

"Yet in all these things we are more than conquerors through Him who loved us." Romans 8:37.

Be Encouraged in the Lord

Anytime you are tempted to shift your focus from God, encourage yourself in the Lord by doing the following:

- Bring to remembrance all the past victories the Lord has given you in previous trials.

- This encourages you to trust God; and that God who did it in the past will also help you in your current trials. The Almighty God says:

"For I know the thoughts that I think toward you, says the Lord, thoughts of peace and not of evil, to give you a future and a hope." Jeremiah 29:11.

- Delve into the word of God, hide it in your heart; then hold on to it as a spiritual Lifeline.

God's Word will build up your faith, and sharpen your spiritual antenna to access God's abundant peace. It will also sustain you in the Christian race. "... faith comes by hearing, and hearing by the word of God." Romans 10:17.

- Hold on to the promises of God which cannot fail. "For all the promises of God in Him are Yes, and in Him Amen." 2 Corinthians 1:20.

- Increase your prayer "fire"! Remember, *"... men always ought to pray and not loose heart"* Luke 18:1.

God's perfect peace

As you trustingly and patiently wait for God; you will be enabled to truly rest in Him. Also, God's perfect peace will fill one's heart. The Bible says:

"You will keep him in perfect peace, whose mind is stayed on You, because he trusts in You." Isaiah 26:3.

Conclusion

In the light of all the above, it is very clear that you cannot be put to shame. This should gladden you, and keep your heart at rest in Him:

"... Who is able to do exceedingly abundantly above all that we ask or think, according to the power that works in us, to Him be glory in the church by Christ Jesus to all generations, forever and ever. Amen." Ephesians 3:20.

22
Be Praise-full

Introduction

As earlier mentioned in this Book, praise is a component of prayers. Therefore, as the Christian engages in warfare in the place of prayers, it must be coupled with the weapon of praise, worship and thanksgiving to the living God.

God dwells in Praise

"... You are holy, enthroned in the praises of Israel." (Psalm 22:3); and Christians are the spiritual Israel.

The Almighty God dwells in the praises of Christians. When we offer sincere praise, worship and thanksgiving to God, we are creating a habitat for God to be enthroned in all His glory and power.

Praising God is a command

Offering praise to God is not optional, but a command; and so Christians don't have a choice in the matter. The Bible says:

"In everything give thanks; for this is the will of God in Christ Jesus for you." 1 Thessalonians 5:18.

Therefore, we are to praise God continually; both when things go the way we want, and vice versa. This honours God, and shows our absolute faith in Him. The Bible admonishes us to:

"... continually offer the sacrifice of praise to God, that is, the fruit of our lips, giving thanks to His name." Hebrews 13:15.

It is very easy to praise God when things go "well" with us, and not during trials; yet, we are to praise Him at all times.

The Holy Spirit's help

Praising God in all situations is impossible in the power of the flesh. However, as we grow in Christ, and key into the Holy Spirit our Helper, He will help us to be thankful in all situations.

Praising God during trials

The case of Paul and Silas recorded in Acts 16:25-34 is a typical example of praising God during moments of trials.

Paul and Silas were imprisoned for the sake of the Gospel (See Acts 16:16-24). While behind bars, the jailer *"put them into the inner prison and fastened their feet in the stocks."* (Acts 16: 24).   Despite the humiliations and sufferings, Paul and Silas were not depressed.

"... at midnight Paul and Silas were praying and singing hymns to God.... Suddenly there was a great earthquake, so that the foundations of the prison were shaken; and immediately all the doors were opened and everyone's chains were loosed." Acts 16:25 & 26.

The Power of Praise

In the light of the above verses, here are some of the things the weapon of praise can accomplish in the place of prayers:

(1). A spiritual earthquake that will shake off all that needs to be shaken off from our lives, Homes,

Ministries; in the lives of people we intercede for, in the Church, and the society. For example, the yoke of sin, toxic friendships and courtships, stronghold of afflictions, generational sins and curses etc.

(2). The shaking and breaking down of all spiritual foundations that represent imprisonment in our lives and situations, in the Church, the society, and our generation.

(3). "Doors" will be opened; that is, all doors that has been closed against us will be flung open as we couple praise with prayers.

(4). "Chains" will be broken. These are spiritual chains which are unseen, but yet are very real; they are highly frustrating and stagnating!

Spiritual Chains tie people down as per their purpose, potentials, progress, health, finances, fruitfulness, joy, fulfilment etc.

When chains are broken, there will be salvation, holiness, restoration, provision, progress, healing, answered prayers, relief and joy. People are thus set free to fulfil God's purpose for their lives.

(5). The power of praise can set the stage for the salvation of souls, as in the case of the jailer and his household (Acts 16:27-34).

High Level Praise and Prayers

As Christians couple prayers with praise, worship and thanksgiving to God, the joy of the Lord fills our hearts. This attracts others to Christ, God's Name is glorified in us; and through us. Some other benefits of praises are:

- It gives our prayers a boost; as in the above-mentioned example of Paul and Silas in Acts 16:25-34.

- The power and glory of God descend. Therefore, afflictions, snares, oppressions, yokes, desolations etc. cannot stay; rather, they are broken and melted under the fire of God's glory and power.

- God's glory rubs on us; and empowers one to live holy. We also receive grace to do exploits for God.

As we couple obedience to God with a lifestyle of praise, we will have joy and all-round good health - spiritually, emotionally and physically.

"A merry heart does good, like medicine, but a broken spirit dries the bones." Proverbs 17:22 .

Conclusion

Being praise-full brings down God's glory; and needs are met when His glory falls. Therefore, we are to continually couple our prayers with quality praise, worship and thanksgiving.

The Almighty God is in control of our lives; and He is able, and willing to turn all situations to our benefits. Knowing this will help us to praise Him at all times;

even when we sometimes don't understand His dealings with us.

Therefore, our lifestyle should be: *"I will bless the Lord at all times; His praise shall continually be in my mouth"* Psalm 34:1.

23

Be Expectant

Introduction

The Almighty God has given a "blank cheque" to all Christians to fill in our requests. He has assured us that we will receive when we ask; and His promises are reliable.

"Ask, and it will be given to you, seek, and you will find; knock, and it will be opened to you. For everyone who asks receives, and he who seeks finds, and to him who knocks it will be opened." Matthew 7:7 & 8.

Also, It is written: *"And whatever things you ask in prayer, believing, you will receive."* Matthew 21:22.

Be Expectant!

As you offer prayers and praises to God, expect to receive answers to your prayers. If your requests align with His will, and you ask with the right motive (not for self-aggrandizement); you will receive much more than you think or expect! Our God is He:

"... Who is able to do exceedingly abundantly above all that we ask or think, according to the power that works in us, to Him be glory in the church by Christ Jesus to all generations, forever and ever. Amen." Ephesians 3:20.

Implications of expecting from God

When you expect God to send answers to your prayers, you are indirectly saying:

- I have no other source of help apart from God.

- My hope is in God and not in man; or man-made gods.

- I have complete confidence in God and His Word.

- I know God is Almighty; and so, nothing is impossible with Him.

- I believe that God cannot lie; He will do whatever He says He will do.

- My mind is at rest in God; no agitations, *no shaking**.

- I have a great trust in God's timing as per the physical manifestation of my prayer requests.

- I know God really loves me; and so, will surely do me good!

Your trust is not misplaced

When Christians are completely dependent on God as we expect answers to our prayers; one cannot be put to shame. The Almighty God says:

"For I know the thoughts that I think toward you, says the Lord, thoughts of peace and not of evil, to give you a future and a hope." Jeremiah 29:11.

Good attitude while waiting

To have a good attitude in the waiting period means: let there be no anxiety, doubts, self-pity, bitterness, envy of others; in short, no manifestation of any negative emotions!

This is not to mean you cannot be honest with God about your pains and concerns. Therefore, if you feel like crying while pouring your heart to God, please, go ahead and do so. The Bible says:

"Trust in Him at all times, you people; pour out your heart before Him; God is a refuge for us." Psalm 62:8.

However, pouring your heart to God ought to be done in quietness of heart; and confidence in Him;

therein lies your strength! *"For thus says the Lord God, the Holy One of Israel... In quietness and confidence shall be your strength.... "* Isaiah 30:15.

Please, be reminded that: *"It is good that one should hope and wait quietly for the salvation of the Lord."* (Lamentations 3:26); thus the peace of God which passes all understanding will fill your heart.

Conclusion

Please, no matter how long the waiting period may seem, don't shift ground in your complete trust in God, and in your expectations from Him.

Therefore, keep trusting; keep expecting; keep serving God with your talents! As you do, the Almighty God will ensure you are not put to shame; He will surely do you good!

"The Lord is good to those who wait for Him, to the soul who seeks Him." Lamentations 3:25.

24
God has the Final Say

Introduction

All power belongs to God; and He has the final say in all things. The Almighty God has power over all His creatures.

"Every living creature is in the hands of God." Job 12:10 (CEV); and *"Known unto God are all His works from the beginning of the world."* Acts 15:18 (KJV).

God does as He pleases

The Almighty God does as He pleases. *"Whatever the Lord pleases He does, in heaven and in earth, in the seas and in all deep places."* Psalm 135:60.

However, we can be assured that He has our best interest at heart in all His dealings with us. God says: *"For I know the thoughts that I think toward you, says the Lord, thoughts of peace and not of evil, to give you a future and a hope."* Jeremiah 29:11.

Things are at God's Discretion

As above-mentioned, God is in control of all things in His Universe, and this includes how He chooses to answer our prayers. That is, God has the final say in the answers He sends in response to our prayers; we should always remember this as we "war" in the prayer closet. The Bible says:

"We humans make plans, but the Lord has the final word." Proverbs 16:1 (CEV).

This understanding will help us to be sincerely joyous and grateful for the outcome of our prayers; especially when it differs from what we feel we want.

God's decision can be trusted

The Almighty God has an amazing love for us, and so will always do us good. Also, God is all-knowing, and He knows the end from the beginning; therefore, we can safely trust Him in all His dealings with us.

"As for God, His way is perfect; the word of the Lord is proven; He is a shield to all who trust in Him." Psalm 18:30.

God is unfathomably rich in wisdom and understanding. He sees the whole picture of things; and so His decisions are reliable.

"Oh, the depth of the riches both of the wisdom and knowledge of God! How unsearchable are His judgements and His ways past finding out!" Romans 11:33.

God gives perfect Gifts

God cares very much about His children that He desires only the best for us at all times. We can therefore be assured that whatever He does in response to our prayers is very perfect; and the best for us.

"For the Lord God is a sun and a shield; the Lord will give grace and glory; no good thing will He withhold from those who walk uprightly. O Lord of hosts, Blessed is the man who trusts in you." Psalm 84:1 & 2.

Conclusion

In the light of all the above, as you go to God in prayers and are expectant, always remember that the final decision rests with Him. You can be assured of His best at all times.

"Now to the King eternal, immortal, invisible, to God Who alone is wise, be honour and glory forever and ever. Amen." 1 Timothy 1:17.

25
God's Timing is Perfect

Introduction

"To everything there is a season, a time for every purpose under heaven." Ecclesiastes 12:1.

The Almighty God has authority over all His creations. He also has the perfect timing for all He does in His Universe, including when to send answers to our prayers.

God and His Timing

God will surely answer our prayers, but in His Own time, not ours! We can be very sure that His timing is perfect, and the best for us. Having this profound trust in God is honouring to Him; and also beneficial to us.

- You will have God's peace and joy; even in the waiting period before the physical manifestation of your prayer requests.

- It will help you not to be discouraged when the answer seems to be longer than expected.

- It will restrain you from "moving ahead of God" to "make" things happen based on your limited understanding. This saves you from messing up things.

Been praying for 'long'?

Perhaps you have been praying to God for a very long time concerning one need or the other in your life, family, or that of a loved one; in the Church, or the larger society?

Maybe you have been trusting God in prayers concerning healing (physical or emotional), spiritual growth, salvation for the unsaved, restoration for the backslider, victory over besetting sins, academic wisdom or progress?

Perhaps it is Ministry Expansion; the much-needed job or promotion, the arrival of those very precious babies, financial provision or breakthrough, God's guidance in your life etc.

Getting discouraged?

You have really trusted and presented your requests to God in prayers, but you are yet to see the physical manifestations; perhaps things "seem" to be getting worse!

Perhaps people are mocking and insulting you, that if your God is powerful, He ought to have helped you. Perhaps this often weigh you down, and you feel hopeless and helpless. Please, be of good courage; do not loose heart, nor be in despair. Persist in prayers against all odds.

The Almighty God will defend His Name in your life. He is working behind the scene on "your file"; to bring forth your testimonies soonest!

God is mindful of you

God has not forgotten you, and can never forget you. He is mindful of your prayers, and your "tears". He knows you by name, and knows your House address; and even if you are homeless, God knows your location.

He knows all you have gone through, or that you are going through. God knows your pains and struggles; and He says:

"Can a woman forget her nursing child, and not have compassion on the son of her womb? Surely they may forget, yet I will not forget you. See I have inscribed you on the palms of My hands; Your walls are continually before Me." Isaiah 49:15 & 16.

Things will soon make sense

God is our caring Heavenly Father, and He is working behind the scene on your behalf. In due time, everything will make sense; all things will work together for your good.

"And we know that all things work together for good to those who love God, to those who are the called according to His purpose." Romans 8:28.

God will not allow you to be stretched beyond what you can bear. Your expected "package" of answered prayers will arrive in the nick of time; at God's Own time!

God will arrive on time

The Almighty God will never come too late, because; *"God is our refuge and strength, a very present help in trouble."* Psalm 46:1.

Therefore, continue to trustingly and patiently wait for Him; you cannot be put to shame. However, remember that our God lives in timelessness; it is here on earth that we count times and seasons.

"But, beloved, do not forget this one thing, that with the Lord one day is as a thousand years, and a thousand years as one day" 2 Peter 3:8.

The prayer points you have been committing to God for about a year in the calendar of the earth may just be like a minute before Him! Therefore, don't relent; rather, increase your prayer fire and trust level.

God's timing is perfect

The Almighty God has the power to do all our prayer requests that align with His will for us. However, as earlier mentioned, He will do it in His Own Time, not ours; and God's timing is very perfect!

Conclusion

These words have been used here as follows:

- Timing: "the choice or judgement of when something should be done". (oxforddictionaries.com).

- Perfect: "faultless, highly suitable for someone; or exactly right". (oxforddictionaries.com).

God's choice or judgement of when to send answers to our prayers is faultless! That is, God's timing is faultless; God's timing is highly suitable and exactly right for us!

26
Victory and Glory are Assured

Introduction

You have prayed! you have praised! you have fasted! you have lived holy! You have lived a fasted life! You have trusted in God, and in His timing! You have been expectant! You have patiently waited!

You have rejoiced in the Lord! You have claimed God's promises! You have wept! You have wondered! Again, you have wondered... how long will it be before the dawn of answered prayers? God's Word says:

"Do not fear, for you will not be ashamed; neither be disgraced, for you will not be put to shame...." Isaiah 54:4a.

Look to God alone

Our only Source of help is the Almighty God; the Creator of Heaven and Earth, the King of all the earth, and Commander- in- Chief of the Heavenly Army. He is also our loving Heavenly Father; and will surely arise for your help.

Therefore, you can boldly say: *"I will lift up my eyes to the hills – from whence comes my help? My help comes from the Lord, Who made heaven and earth."* Psalm 121:1 & 2.

God will help you

The Almighty God will arise for your help, and make all things (your trials, challenges; even your mistakes etc.) to work together for your good; both in this world, and in eternity.

The joy of answered prayers will surely come; so be encouraged to keep praying until your joy is full. *"...

Weeping may endure for a night, but joy comes in the morning." Psalm 30:5b.

No defeat, No shame!

God will not allow you to suffer defeat; He will give you Victory! God's word of assurance is:*"They will fight you, but they will not defeat you. I am with you, and I will rescue you....* Jeremiah 1:19. (GW).

Also, God will not allow you to be ashamed, He will give you Glory! The Almighty God says: *"... they shall not be ashamed who wait for Me."* Isaiah 49: 23c.

Conclusion

In view of the above, it is certain that the Almighty God will give you Victory and Glory; so you can joyfully declare:

"In my distress I called upon the Lord, and cried out to my God; He heard my voice from His temple, and my cry entered His ears." Psalm 22:7.

"Blessed be the Lord, because He has heard the voice of my supplications! The Lord is my strength and my shield; my heart trusted in Him, and I am helped; Therefore my heart greatly rejoices, and with my song I will praise Him." Psalm 28: 6 & 7.

27
God Loves You

The Almighty God loves you! God cares very much about you, that He specially "wrapped" a precious Gift for you (and all mankind); and this is the Gift of Salvation.

"For God so loved the world that He gave His only begotten Son, that whoever believes in Him should not perish but have everlasting life. For God did not send His Son into the world to condemn the world, but that the world through Him might be saved." John 3:16 & 17.

Why this Gift?

God packaged the Salvation Gift because of His great love for you (and all mankind); so that you can be delivered from the bondage of sin.

"For all have sinned and fall short of the glory of God." (Romans 3:23); and *"... the wages of sin is death, but the gift of God is eternal life in Christ Jesus our Lord."* Romans 6:23.

When one receives this "Gift", and holds on to it till the end of one's life through a life of holiness; you will gain eternal life.

Have you received the Gift?

My dearly beloved reader, have you received God's Gift of Salvation through Jesus Christ? If yes, please, accept my Congratulations. I have received God's Salvation Gift too; and for this, I am very glad.

In appreciation of God's great love for us, let us continue to live for God till the end; this will guarantee us eternal life. It is very important that we tell others how to receive this precious Gift too.

A Backslider?

Perhaps you have received Jesus Christ as your personal Lord and Saviour before now, but you have gone back into your "vomit"; your former sins. This is very risky! Quickly come back to your first love for Christ. He will not cast you away.

Genuinely repent from sin, ask God to forgive you; and rededicate your life to Jesus Christ <u>Now</u>!

"Seek the Lord while He may be found, call upon Him while He is near. Let the wicked forsake his way, and the unrighteous man his thoughts; let him return to the Lord, and He will have mercy on him; and to our God, for He will abundantly pardon." Isaiah 55:6 & 7.

Not yet born again?

If you have <u>not</u> received God's Salvation Gift, please, urgently do so. Don't delay; because this is very dangerous. *"... Behold, now is the accepted time; behold, now is the day of salvation."* 2 Corinthians 6:2.

Flee for your precious soul now!

- Be sincerely ready to repent from sins, and also to forsake them.

"He who covers his sins will not prosper, but whoever confesses and forsakes them will have mercy." Proverbs 28:13.

- Confess your sins to God; and ask Him to forgive you.

"If we confess our sins, He is faithful and just to forgive us our sin and to cleanse us from all unrighteousness." 1 John 1:9.

- Accept Jesus Christ as your personal Lord and Saviour.

"Behold, I stand at the door and knock. If anyone hears My voice and opens the door, I will come in to him and dine with him, and he with Me." Revelation 3:20.

Please, don't delay; grab the opportunity now and get born again! A time is coming when it will be too late, and you don't know when this may be. Therefore, *"Today, if you will hear His voice, do not harden your hearts."* Hebrews 4:7.

If you have sincerely taken the above steps, please, accept my hearty Congratulations. *See the Appendix for 'Now that you are born again';* it contains tips on what to do to help you grow in Christ.

Once again, Congratulations.

JESUS IS COMING SOON
(Revelation 22:12)

APPENDIX

Now That you are Born Again

Congratulations on your decision to truly repent from your sin and receive Jesus Christ as your personal Lord and Saviour; that is, you are born again. This means you are saved from the dangers and punishment of sin. You are now a child of God.

"... As many as received Him, to them He gave the right to become children of God, to those who believe in His name; who were born, not of blood, nor of the will of the flesh, nor of the will of man, but of God." John 1:12 & 13.

What a great privilege to be a child of God; the Prince or Princess of the King of all the earth, and the King of all kings!

Assurance of Salvation

It is very important for you to firmly believe that God has forgiven you your sins; and so you should no longer feel guilty or sad over your past. God says: The Almighty God assures us that: *"If we confess our sins, He is faithful and just to forgive us our sins and to cleanse us from all unrighteousness."* 1 John 1:9.

The Help of the Holy Spirit

When a person becomes truly born again, the Holy Spirit comes to live in him or her; to guide and help in the Christian race. Our Lord Jesus Christ says:

"And I will pray the Father, and He will give you another Helper, that He may abide with you forever – the Spirit of truth, whom the world cannot receive, because it neither sees Him nor knows Him; but you know Him, for He dwells with you and will be in you." John 14:16 & 17.

Therefore, be assured that the Holy Spirit is with you; He is also in you to help you – both in the good and challenging seasons of life. The Bible says:

"... when He, the Spirit of truth has come, He will guide you into all truth; ... and He will tell you things to come." John 16:13.

He will help you to run the Christian race successfully to the end; just don't turn your back on Christ. For your sustenance in Christ, ensure that you continually obey the Holy Spirit, your Helper.

Tips on Christian Growth

Salvation is the beginning of a life-long journey with Christ Jesus. God wants you to grow in your new relationship with Christ; and here are some tips on achieving this.

(1). Please, get your own copy of the Holy Bible; a daily devotional that is based on the true Word of

God, and a notebook to jot down the lessons you learn daily from the Bible.

(2). Read your Bible every day; study it, and meditate on the lessons learnt.

"As newborn babes, desire the pure milk of the Word, that you may grow thereby." 1 Peter 2:2. (See also Joshua 1:8).

(3). Obey God's Word. God says, *"If you love Me, keep My commandments." John 14:15.* (See also John 15:14).

(4). Pray every day. *"Pray without ceasing."* 1 Thessalonians 5:17.

(5). Fellowship with other Christians where the undiluted Word of God is preached and practiced.

"And let us not neglect our meeting together, as some people do, but encourage one another, especially now that the day of His return is drawing near." Hebrews 10:25(NLT).

(6). Share with others how they can receive God's Salvation Gift. Our Lord Jesus Christ says:

"... All authority has been given to Me in heaven and on earth. "Go therefore and make disciples of all the nations, baptizing them in the name of the Father and of the Son and of the Holy Spirit, teaching them to observe all things I have commanded you; and lo I am

with you always, even to the end of the age." Amen." Matthew 28:18 – 20.

Tell others how they can repent from sin, and receive Jesus Christ as their Lord and Saviour. Also, follow them up to stand for Christ; so they too can go out to win others for Christ. This is called Evangelism and Discipleship; and they are two sides of the same coin.

This is the Assignment Jesus Christ gave to His disciples throughout all ages; and when you are actively and consistently involved, God will be happy with you. Failure to do this very important Assignment will make God unhappy with you! This is because God:

"... desires all men to be saved and come to the knowledge of the truth." 1 Timothy 2:4.

It is not surprising therefore that the Bible says; *"... he who wins soul is wise."* (Proverbs 11:20); you make God happy, and your own soul is preserved.

(7). Expect the second coming of Jesus Christ, living each moment as if Christ will come that very moment. *"And everyone who has this hope in Him purifies himself, just as He is pure."* 1 John 3:3.

"The grace of the Lord Jesus Christ, and the love of God, and the communion of the Holy Spirit be with you all. Amen." 2 Corinthians 13:14.

Other Books by the Author

1. The Complete Woman

3. A Tasty Meal for the Man of Taste (Guidelines on Overcoming Sexual Temptations)

4. Building Your Home for God's glory (Gems from the Life of Nehemiah)

5. Teenage Friendship (A Guide to Healthy Social Relations)

6. Dynamics of Marital Harmony

7. A Place of Beauty and Satisfaction

8. Ibugbe Ewa ati Itelorun (Yoruba version of 6 above)

9. Thy Will be Done (Biblical Guidelines on choosing a Life Partner)

10. Oneness not Sameness (Tips for Harmony in the Home)

11. Rescue them From the Fire (A Call to Aggressive Evangelism/Follow-up)

12. The Whole Duty of Man

13. This Faith is Real

14. Igbagbo Yi Daju (Yoruba version of 12 above)

15. Flee This Plague Now

16. In Quietness and Confidence (Gems from the

Information about the Ministry

The Maranatha Ambassadors is a non-denominational Christian Organisation committed to the propagation of the Gospel of our Lord Jesus Christ. To achieve this, we currently offer the following services:

Evangelistic Outreaches, Family Harmony Crusades, Children and Teens' Concerns, Youth Mentoring, Free Counselling Services; Sale of Bibles, Christian Literatures, CD's, Gift items etc.; Publication of Christian Books and Tracts.

MARANATHA BIBLE CLUB: Free for children and young adults. Meeting Time is 4pm – 5pm every Saturday at the Ministry's premises.

LIFEGATE CRECHE: Affordable Baby-care and Playgroup services. We provide a physically and spiritually healthy atmosphere where parents can restfully keep their children while away to work.

DOMINION CHRISTIAN BOOKSHOP: We stock and sell different versions of the Holy Bible, colourfully illustrated children's bibles, christian books (for children, young adults and Adults), christian audio and video CD's, tambourines, gift items, toys etc. at affordable costs.

Invitation for Programmes

We accept invitations from Churches, Christian Organisations and Fellowship Groups; to conduct Seminars for youths and children; also to give Talks on Youth Work, How to handle Children Ministry; and on the Christian life generally (See our contact details below).

Counselling Needed?

Are you burdened, troubled, confused, or traumatized? Perhaps you are beaten, battered, and shattered; and you need an empathetic and non-judgemental listener?

Perhaps you want to know about God's plan of salvation for mankind; or you are thirsty for more of God?

Please, feel free to talk to us at:

The Maranatha Ambassadors,

Plot 13, Bajowa Way, Off El-Shaddai Road,

Opposite the New Royal Birds Hotel &Towers,

Alagbaka G.R.A., Akure. Ondo State. Nigeria.

Email: themaranathaambassadors@gmail.com

Tel. +2348038041113.

If you have just been born again, or just rededicated your life to Jesus Christ; or you have been blessed through this book, we will be glad to hear your testimony.

Postscript

We are glad to inform you of some changes in the Ministry's identity as follows:

(1). The Ministry is now to be known as **The Maranatha Ambassadors**. Our Anchor verse is:

"Now then, we are ambassadors for Christ, as though God were pleading through us: we implore you on Christ's behalf, be reconciled to God." 2 Corinthians 5:20.

However, our mission statement remains the same, which is: **Preparing Souls for the Soon-coming King.**

(2). The publishing arm is now called **Jochebed Publishing House**; while its motto is still: **Reaching Souls with the Bread of Life**.

(3). All other departments of the Ministry remain the same.

(4). *"Brethren, pray for us."* 1 Thessalonians 5:25.